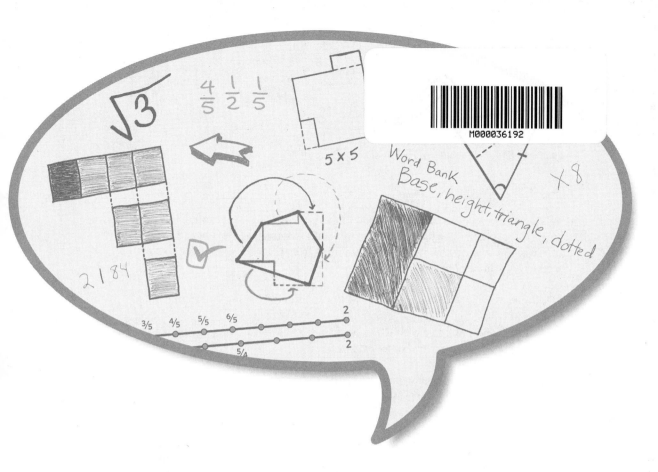

# Mathematical Thinking
## *and* Communication

## *Access for English Learners*

**MARK DRISCOLL**
**JOHANNAH NIKULA**
**JILL NEUMAYER DePIPER**

Heinemann
Portsmouth, NH

**Heinemann**
361 Hanover Street
Portsmouth, NH 03801–3912
www.heinemann.com

*Offices and agents throughout the world*

Fostering Mathematics Success of English Language Learners Project (FMSELL) was supported by the DRK12 Program, National Science Foundation, through Grant DRL-0821950 to the Education Development Center, Inc. Mathematics Coaching Supporting English Learners Project (MCSEL) was supported by the Institute of Education Sciences, U.S. Department of Education, through Grant R305A110076 to the Education Development Center, Inc. The opinions expressed in this book are those of the authors and do not represent views of the National Science Foundation, the Institute of Education Sciences, or the U.S. Department of Education.

Cataloging-in-Publication Data is on file with the Library of Congress.

ISBN: 978-0-325-07477-1

Editor: Katherine Bryant
Production editor: Sonja S. Chapman
Typesetter: Cape Cod Compositors, Inc.
Cover and interior designs: Catherine Arakelian
Manufacturing: Veronica Bennett

Printed in the United States of America on acid-free paper

20  19  18  17  16  EBM  1  2  3  4  5

# Contents

---

**How to Access the Online
Professional Development Resources**

Step 1: Go to www.heinemann.com

Step 2: Click on "Login" to open or create your account. Enter your email address and password, or click "Create a New Account" to set up an account.

Step 3: Enter keycode MTACPD and click "Register."

---

# Acknowledgments

The authors are grateful to the many people whose work with us over the past decade helped shape the ideas expressed in this book. The bulk of this support came in two research projects, Fostering Mathematics Success of English Language Learners Project (FMSELL) and Mathematics Coaching Supporting English Learners Project (MCSEL).[1] We want to acknowledge the very helpful support of the program officers of these projects: Julio Lopez-Ferrao for FMSELL, at National Science Foundation, and Karen Douglas for MCSEL, at Institute of Education Sciences.

In one, the other, or both of these two projects, we were joined by a wonderful team of EDC colleagues: David Bamat, Rebecca Bangura, Enrique Colon-Baco, Roser Gine, Grace Kelemanik, Maria Teresa Sanchez, Peter Tierney-Fife, and Rachel Wing DiMatteo. We were fortunate to collaborate with our partners from Horizon Research, Inc., a team led by Daniel J. Heck, on the FMSELL project. Contributing skillfully to our research and development on the MCSEL project was our research consultant, Kathryn Race of Race and Associates. We were wisely guided in the work of these projects by advisors and evaluators including Harold Asturias, Kathryn Chval, Marta Civil, Megan Franke, Helena Miranda, Judit Moschkovitch, John Moyer, Andrew Porter, Nora Ramirez, and Judith Zawojewski.

---

[1] Fostering Mathematics Success of English Language Learners Project (FMSELL) was supported by the DRK12 Program, National Science Foundation, through Grant DRL-0821950 to the Education Development Center, Inc. Mathematics Coaching Supporting English Learners Project (MCSEL) was supported by the Institute of Education Sciences, U.S. Department of Education, through Grant R305A110076 to the Education Development Center, Inc. The opinions expressed in this book are those of the authors and do not represent views of the National Science Foundation, the Institute of Education Sciences, or the U.S. Department of Education.

Across both projects, we worked with several hundred mathematics teachers and coaches in thirteen states, whose commitment to improving mathematics access for students who are English learners was inspiring and enlightening.

Finally, during the past decade, we also conducted several professional-development projects with New York City's Office of English Language Learners. We are grateful to Maria Santos, then director of OELL, her staff, and the mathematics coaches, ESL specialists, and mathematics teachers of New York City for helping us realize that, working together, teams of educators within a school can transform the teaching of mathematics for English learners.

# Introduction

"Words create worlds, he used to tell me when I was a child. They must be used very carefully. Some words, once having been uttered, gain eternity and can never be withdrawn."

—Susannah Heschel, daughter of Rabbi Abraham Heschel[1]

Laments about the state of American schools seem to occur frequently in the popular press. District, state, and federal mandates often follow. And when the articles and mandates turn to potential solutions, these solutions often sound like zero-sum, or win-lose, propositions, with underlying messages that can be heard, particularly by teachers, as, "In order for all students to make gains, teachers must do more." From our work with teachers, coaches, and schools, we believe that better solutions are those that are win-win, with teachers doing what they signed up for in the first place when they entered the teaching profession. In particular, we want teachers to gain as students gain, with "better" solutions arising from teachers doing familiar things perhaps *differently*, rather than "better" solutions being equated with teachers layering *more* onto what they have been doing.

The key, we believe, is to remember that students, particularly English learners (ELs), are *thinking* when they engage in mathematics tasks and, moreover, using language as they think. What if that thinking could be made visible and audible and caused to blossom into productive

---

[1] A. J. Heschel and S. Heschel, *Moral Grandeur and Spiritual Audacity* (New York: Farrar, Straus, and Giroux, 1996), ix–x.

mathematical practices and mathematical communication? That would benefit students while benefiting teachers. Right there would be a win-win solution, and it would emanate from mathematics tasks already used or tasks similar to those already used. We argue in this book that familiar tasks can be enhanced for ELs with listening/reading supports and speaking/writing prompts, along with prompts for ELs to use mathematical visual representations to propel and communicate their thinking.

To move from the status quo to the win-win solution, mathematics teachers of ELs have particular challenges to overcome, especially two commonly held opinions. First, there is a widespread belief that students need English proficiency in order to do mathematics reasoning tasks. A related conviction holds that the best way to create access to mathematics tasks for ELs is to lighten the cognitive demand of the tasks. Neither the "English first" nor the "lighten the cognitive demand" strategies about mathematics tasks for English learners is necessary for building proficiency in mathematical reasoning. Instead, we suggest remembering that ELs are thinking when working on mathematics tasks, and by letting that thinking become more visible and audible, teachers can nurture the productive potential in that thinking, as well as help adjust any faulty or misinformed thinking.

This book is intended to be a resource for mathematics teachers whose students include ELs. Furthermore, because this book explores the roles that language plays in the learning of mathematics, we also believe it can be useful to all teachers of mathematics, regardless of the particular collection of students in their classrooms. But these strategies, tailored in ways to meet the needs of different students, are absolutely essential for ELs. To meet ELs' needs it is necessary to nurture mathematics teaching practices that "specifically address the language demands of students who are developing skill in listening, speaking, reading, and writing in a second language while learning mathematics" (Celedón-Pattichis and Ramirez 2012, 1). In other words, although ELs must gain facility in using English to express themselves mathematically, in order to succeed in mathematics, the learning can and should happen "while learning mathematics."

When we talk about ELs, we mean students for whom English is not their home or first language and whose current English language proficiency level potentially interferes with their grade-level mathematics work. ELs, like other students, are by no means all the same, and each brings different strengths and struggles to the classroom. We recognize the importance of attending to (1) students' different English-language proficiency levels, cultural backgrounds, schooling backgrounds, first languages, current mathematical understanding, and so on, and (2) classrooms' different makeups in regard to the mix of EL and non-EL students as well as the background of EL students in the class. We intend this book to be useful for all teachers in thinking about supporting the ELs they happen to teach.

## Background to Our Work

This book grows out of a decade of work with mathematics teachers of ELs, in a wide range of districts—including large urban, small urban, suburban, and rural. The first languages of ELs in these districts were both numerous and varied, as were the policies created to serve their needs. That set of experiences allowed us to hone a set of ideas and strategies to increase access to mathematics learning opportunities in English-speaking classrooms. The ideas and strategies were mainly tested in middle-grade classrooms, but we believe they can be adapted to both lower and higher grades.

Our interest in working with mathematics teachers of ELs began a decade ago in New York City. We were asked to conduct a seminar series, with an emphasis on analyzing student work on challenging mathematics tasks. The invited school teams were focused on improving the mathematics performance of English learners in their middle schools. Each team included an ESL specialist, so the teams were well advised in the English-as-second-language needs of EL students. We were not asked there because they thought us knowledgeable about those needs. While relieved about that point, our team still felt a bit at sea and disconnected from participant needs, since we had so little experience working with ELs at that point.

This uneasiness dissolved quickly for us in the early weeks of the project, when the director of the New York City Office of English Language Learners came to a seminar and addressed the participating school teams with words to the effect of:

> For English learners to succeed in learning mathematics, they need to be more *productive* in mathematics classrooms—reasoning more, speaking more, writing more, drawing more.

For our team leading the seminars, this statement had a liberating effect by enabling us to recognize that, as people with experience helping others reason more, speak more, write more, and draw more in mathematics, we did have much to contribute to the efforts of the school teams. This was a major mind-set shift.

In that vein, and briefly put, this book is designed to make a case for mathematics teachers and coaches to secure a similar mind-set. We want teachers and coaches to recognize that their accumulated knowledge and skill in helping students be more productive during mathematics lessons also apply to meeting the learning needs of EL students, albeit, with some targeted shifts in strategy, so that language supports and visual representations can play salient roles. Of course, such a belief would do no good unless put into practice. And so, the book offers ways in which we believe teachers can enrich their current practice to create access for EL students to proficiency in mathematical reasoning and development of mathematical practices.

# Guiding Perspectives

We outline below four perspectives that have guided our own work and the work of our collaborating teachers. We hope they will be useful to you in your own efforts to improve access to proficiency in mathematical reasoning and development of mathematical practices among ELs. Underlying the perspectives is an assumption about teaching and teacher learning: We assume that the vast majority of teachers would very much like to devote time to activities that provide them enjoyable and useful learning, including new ways to think about mathematics, about language, and about relationships between mathematics and language. These activities might plumb the depths of potential in mathematical visual representations; provide ideas and strategies useful to engage hard-to-reach students; and invite collaborative, professional problem solving. At the same time, we recognize that many other, often-mandated, activities can make time scarce for our suggested professional development. Therefore, we offer in this book ideas, activities, and strategies in the hopes that they can be employed when windows of time do open up.

The guiding perspectives are that we mathematics educators should:

1. **Adopt useful, actionable definitions of equity.** Defining equity can be an elusive task. It cannot mean "equal treatment for all," because that could never be achieved in a world where material and financial resources are distributed so unevenly. Thus, that definition just does not seem practical. Another definition candidate, "A fair chance for everyone," appears to pass the practical test, but the word *fair* requires unpacking. In our experience, *access* is a key piece of fairness, that is, providing each learner alternative ways to achieve, no matter the particular obstacles he or she faces. A related piece is *potential*, as in the

potential shown by students to do challenging mathematical reasoning and problem solving. Seeing fairness in terms of access and potential can give more concrete meaning to "fairness for all" as groundwork for equity.

These words all prompt wondering—in the case of *access*, about what is currently missing, and in the case of *potential*, about what might be done next to create access. They invite problem solving to find ways around obstacles in the path of student growth. For instance, what stands in the way of ELs' becoming proficient in solving mathematical word problems? To a large extent, the words in the problems constitute the obstacle. One alternate access route could involve visual representations, especially if they are complemented by a set of carefully matched language strategies. Similarly, when ELs or other students struggle to solve a mathematical task and show evidence of potentially proficient thinking, what stands in the way of their developing robust mathematical practices, as described in the Common Core Standards of Mathematical Practice? One likely stumbling point is a curriculum that is overloaded with computational procedures. With this in mind, we have advocated students to engage with geometric reasoning tasks as an access route toward fulfilling potential in mathematical practices.

2. **Take an expansive view of the role of language in mathematics and in teaching mathematics.** In his book, *The Language of Mathematics*,[2] Barton writes, "Mathematical concepts, objects, and relationships arise through language, and within particular socio-cultural environments, in response to human thinking about quantity, relationships, and space" (88). Given this intimate relationship between mathematics and language, and given the pervasive importance of quantity, relationships, and space in mathematics, it makes sense that all teachers, but especially teachers of English learners, would want to develop habits of heightened attention to language. An example related to this point comes from our work on fostering geometric thinking,[3] where we videotaped three eighth graders working on one of our geometric dissection problems. In the problem, the students were asked to come up

---

[2] Bill Barton, *The Language of Mathematics: Telling Mathematical Tales* (New York: Springer Science+Business Media, 2009).

[3] M. Driscoll, R. Wing DiMatteo, J. Nikula, and M. Egan, *Fostering Geometric Thinking* (Portsmouth, NH: Heinemann, 2007).

with a method to dissect a provided parallelogram and move the pieces to make a rectangle. The last question was: "Will your method work for any parallelogram?" One of the students drew a parallelogram, tried the method, and declared, "It works!" A second student objected, "But there are other parallelograms," to which the first student asked, "*What other parallelograms?*" The other student fell silent, apparently not knowing how to respond.

After several viewings of this segment, we concluded that the student who objected took "any" to mean what was intended—namely, a synonym for "every." The first student, on the other hand, seemed to interpret "any" in the way it is used in a sentence, like "Do you have any opinion about where to go for lunch?" In this case, one opinion suffices as a response. In mathematics, however, "any" usually has a privileged meaning: every. There are many such instances of words and phrases with privileged meanings in mathematics, and so it behooves all of us to be alert to the use of language in mathematical matters.

3. **Take an expanded view of mathematical proficiency, emphasizing the quality of mathematical thinking.** To some, the advent of the Common Core Standards of Mathematical Practice has presented yet another hurdle for English learners on the road to mathematics proficiency. We have come to recognize, however, that one can look at the eight Standards of Mathematical Practice (SMP) as a lens on EL student potential for mathematical growth and as pointers for teachers toward providing access for EL students to mathematical growth. In Chapter 3 of this book, we discuss our use of a particular problem in our research with English learners: *Rita has read 224 pages of her book. She has $1/5$ of the book left to read. What is the total number of pages in the book?* Several of the students drew a diagram like this:

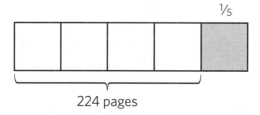

This looks very promising, pointing toward possible next steps of

1. dividing 224 by 4 to get 56

2. recognizing that 56 pages are in each of the four white parts, so

3. there also must be 56 pages in the shaded part. Hence,

4. the total number of pages is 224 + 56 = 280 pages.

These students did none of this, just leaving the diagram they'd constructed. They appeared stuck.

Although they may have been several steps from solution, their record of thinking shows strong potential related to SMP 2: *Reason abstractly and quantitatively*, because they have portrayed diagrammatically the relationship between the quantity "pages read" and the quantity "pages left to read." Furthermore, there is an implicit representation of the relationship between the numbers $1/5$ and $4/5$. A teacher might seize on this evidence of potential to ask questions to advance the student thinking, such as "In your diagram, why are there four parts for 224 pages?" "How many pages in each of the four parts?"

When measured by the gauge "Did they get it?" the answer is sometimes no, but often students' work reveals evidence of SMP potential. We can use that evidence to move the students forward by recognizing it and asking helpful questions to advance thinking.

4. **Keep evidence of student mathematical thinking and communication at the center of focus, and use mathematics tasks that allow this focus.** Student and teacher learning opportunities will thrive when mathematical tasks are employed that elicit student thinking and communication and create records of student thinking and communication, and when teachers' planning around tasks is informed by attention to use of language. In this book, we reflect a strong belief we gained from our work and from reading the research literature in mathematics education: All students benefit from a steady diet of tasks that elicit mathematical reasoning. These tasks can prompt problem solving, analytical reasoning, spatial/geometric reasoning, or quantitative reasoning. Chapter 1 provides examples of each.

The material in this book reflects these perspectives, and we hope that it supports you in adopting them as well. Chapter 1 looks very closely at the topic of access for English learners, with particular attention on access to several ways of reasoning in mathematics; Chapter 2 focuses on the roles mathematical visual representations play in providing ELs access to mathematical thinking and communication; Chapter 3 describes the rationale for teacher analysis of ELs' visual representations as a means to tap EL student potential, along with a framework for analysis; Chapter 4 looks closely at what is meant by learning to communicate mathematically while doing and learning mathematics; Chapter 5 considers the qualities that make tasks conducive to expanding access for EL students; Chapter 6 describes instructional routines that can embed tasks in lessons so that EL access is maximized; and finally, Chapter 7 summarizes major ideas in the book and contains suggestions for ways to start implementing the ideas in your practice.

# Chapter 1

# Creating Access to Mathematics for English Learners

The notion of *access* has been an important beacon for us in our work alongside teachers of students who are English learners. ELs may face many challenges that can impede success in learning mathematics. After we identify these challenges, we seek avenues of access so students can surmount the challenges, building on their strengths as often as possible. Access to the academic English used in instruction, textbooks, and tests is essential, of course, but so is access to opportunities to solve problems and reason mathematically even before students gain high levels of English proficiency.

## How Language Is Involved in Mathematical Reasoning

Our efforts to broaden access proceed along the following line of reasoning:

- Language is deeply involved in the learning of mathematics. At the same time,

- English proficiency is *not* a prerequisite for doing mathematical work that is cognitively demanding, such as reasoning and problem solving. That is because

- Mathematical visual representations and other thinking tools and language tools can be employed to support the integration of academic English into mathematical reasoning and problem solving.

This line of reasoning may challenge beliefs and defy expectations for some and so deserves further unpacking. Suppose a mathematics problem is presented to students. Ideally, most of the students' efforts will include productive struggle with the mathematics, with some beginning "stuff" up front and some closing "stuff" at the end. The productive mathematical struggle in the middle is, for the most part, internal, silent, and driven by previous experience, so it usually doesn't require knowledge of English.

However, the beginning "stuff" (the white rectangle on the left) is the entry door into the task, requiring students' efforts to *make meaning* of the presented task; meanwhile, the "stuff" at the end (the white rectangle on the right) consists of students *communicating* how they reasoned about the task. Students may go back and forth between productive struggle about the mathematics and communicating how they reasoned about that mathematics, thus the cyclical arrows. Both the beginning work to gain access to the task and the later work to communicate based on the productive struggle with the mathematics are wedded to use of written and spoken language.

For example, imagine that the students are presented with a written word problem, and suppose further that the teacher has asked students to cap their mathematical work on the problem by explaining to a partner how they reasoned and solved the problem.

In this case, the challenges in the beginning stuff might be confusing words and phrases in the problem statement or general difficulty tracking the narrative in the problem statement, perhaps because of an unfamiliar context. Also, ELs (like other students) may be looking for cues that tell them to add, subtract, multiply, or divide. This is usually a waste of attention, since words like *more* may signify the need to add but could also involve multiplication or even subtraction. Challenges in the right side of the rectangle may include anxiety about writing an explanation—how to use precise language and full sentences, for example. Also challenging can be the task of translating words in the problem to symbols used in thinking about solving it. Finally, ELs may be especially challenged in attaching words to how they were thinking and what decisions they made along the way.

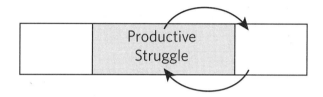

## Cognitive Load and Cognitive Overload

Clearly, this "stuff" before and after the mathematical thinking can trip up ELs, often pushing them into what is called "cognitive overload." The concept of *cognitive load* refers to work the brain does when processing information, within the limits of working memory. Research shows that working memory is limited in how much information it can hold at any one time.[1] Hence, cognitive *overload* can happen quickly—with working memory buckling under too much information to process in too short a time. Returning to the word-problem example: All students, to varying degrees, struggle to do the mathematical work required by problems; however, working memory in ELs is strained even further by language demands, in struggles to draw meaning from problem statements, as well as later in communicating reasoning to others.

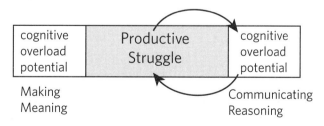

---

[1]  J. Sweller, "Cognitive Load During Problem Solving: Effects on Learning," *Cognitive Science* 12 (1988): 257–85.

### Supports to Reduce Cognitive Load

On the basis of our work with schools, we are convinced that lack of English language proficiency need not preclude ELs from productive struggle with challenging mathematics tasks (involving reasoning and problem solving), *provided* appropriate thinking and language tools are used to support ELs in gaining access to the task and in communicating their thinking about the task—i.e., the "stuff" that comes before and after productive struggle. A key aspect of "appropriate" that we emphasize is that the tools are woven seamlessly into students' implementation of the mathematics tasks. Furthermore, we believe that all students—not just ELs—can benefit from using them. Appropriate tools include mathematical diagrams for word problems, enhanced geometric drawings for geometric reasoning tasks, language access strategies for analyzing the meaning in the wording of tasks, and language production strategies for helping students communicate their mathematical thinking. Examples appear throughout the rest of this chapter and the book.

## Types of Mathematical Reasoning

Our work has involved using tasks to help students—especially ELs—engage with different kinds of mathematical productive struggle. We aim to promote both mathematical problem solving and analytic reasoning, and we focus on contexts that allow spatial/geometric reasoning and quantitative reasoning. These four categories are by no means mutually exclusive. In fact, you will see examples of tasks and student work in this book for which you might rightly say, "That seems like a combination of problem solving and geometric reasoning," or "On that task, students seemed to be using analytic reasoning and quantitative reasoning to support their problem solving." Before we show examples of each of the categories, here are brief definitions.

### Problem Solving

We think of mathematical problem solving as an umbrella that involves careful strategizing and can include the other kinds of mathematical reasoning we describe below. The 2012 What Works Clearinghouse practice guide publication, *Improving Mathematical Problem Solving in Grades 4 Through 8*, says that mathematical problem solving "involves reasoning and analysis, argument construction, and the development of innovative strategies" (6).

The guide lays out research-based arguments and evidence regarding access for all students to proficiency in mathematical problem solving. Among the principal recommendations was regular classroom use of visual representations, such as diagrams: "Students who learn to visually represent the mathematical information in problems prior to writing an equation are more effective at problem solving" (Woodward et al. 2012, 23).[2] This, of course, is a recommendation for all students, but teachers of ELs should see the additional benefits for non-English speakers. In creating and analyzing diagrams and in manipulating geometric drawings, ELs can propel their mathematical thinking, as well as *reveal* their mathematical thinking to teachers, with minimal need to understand English. Furthermore, for mathematical word problems, diagrams can act as a bridge between the words of the problem and the symbolic calculations needed to determine a solution. In the words of one of our collaborating teachers, describing ELs' use of diagrams: "It is just worth everything because it gives them some way to access it and some way to get success."

## Analytic Reasoning

Broadly speaking, analytic reasoning "refers to a set of processes for identifying the causes of events" (Siegler 2003).[3] As a form of mathematical thinking, it involves "distinguishing between features that typically accompany the use of a particular mathematical problem solving technique, and features that are essential for the technique to apply, (and) usually requires analysis of why the technique is appropriate or inappropriate" (229).

Analytic reasoning complements problem solving by broadening students' thinking about problem-solving strategies and by helping them

---

[2]  J. Woodward, S. Beckmann, M. Driscoll, M. Franke, P. Herzig, A. Jitendra, K. R. Koedinger, and P. Ogbuehi, *Improving Mathematical Problem Solving in Grades 4 Through 8: Practice Guide* (NCEE 2012-4055) (Washington, DC: National Center for Education Evaluation and Regional Assistance, Institute of Education Sciences, U.S. Department of Education, 2012). Retrieved from http://ies.ed.gov/ncee/wwc/publications_reviews.aspx#pubsearch/.

[3]  R. S. Siegler, "Implications of Cognitive Science Research for Mathematics Education," in *A Research Companion to Principles and Standards for School Mathematics*, eds. J. Kilpatrick, W. B. Martin, and D. E. Schifter (Reston, VA: National Council of Teachers of Mathematics, 2003), 219–33.

transfer their problem-solving skills to unfamiliar situations, as described by Siegler:[4]

> Encouraging children to explain other people's reasoning in many contexts may lead children to internalize such an analytic stance to the point where they ask such questions reflexively, even when not prompted to do so. . . . When children are actively engaged in understanding why things work the way they do, transfer follows naturally and without great effort.

## Spatial/Geometric Reasoning

By spatial/geometric reasoning, we mean reasoning about properties of geometric figures, reasoning about relationships between geometric figures, and reasoning about geometric measurement in figures, such as perimeter, area, and volume.

In 2008, we completed the Fostering Geometric Thinking project.[5] Two related discoveries in this research and development project were:

- Very many middle graders do not have opportunities to do spatial/geometric reasoning tasks.

- When students do get such opportunities, many (including many ELs) show themselves proficient.

Consequently, we believe spatial/geometric reasoning should have a prominent place in middle-grades classrooms. In his book *The Language of Mathematics*,[6] Barton nicely traces the interactions of language development and mathematical understanding, writing that "mathematical concepts, objects, and relationships arise through language, and within particular socio-cultural environments, in response to human thinking about quantity, relationships, and space" (88). This perspective led us to emphasize the language of quantities, relationships, and space in the shaping of our language strategies. We reason that this emphasis provides a very useful foundation to the full body of language used in mathematical communication and

---

[4]  R. S. Siegler, "Implications of Cognitive Science Research for Mathematics Education," 229.

[5]  M. Driscoll, R. Wing DiMatteo, J. Nikula, M. Egan, J. Mark, and G. Kelemanik, *The Fostering Geometric Thinking Toolkit: A Guide for Staff Development* (Portsmouth, NH: Heinemann, 2008). M. Driscoll, R. Wing DiMatteo, J. Nikula, and M. Egan, *Fostering Geometric Thinking: A Guide for Teachers* (Portsmouth, NH: Heinemann, 2007). Both are products of Fostering Geometric Thinking in the Middle Grades Project (National Science Foundation ESI-0353409). Opinions expressed in this book are those of the authors and not necessarily the opinions of the National Science Foundation.

[6]  B. Barton, *The Language of Mathematics: Telling Mathematical Tales* (New York: Springer Science+Business Media, 2009).

that mathematics teachers can make comfortable and profitable use of this foundation.

In the view of many American mathematics educators, including us, little reasoning is demanded in the geometry tasks that our middle school students see too frequently. For example, if "area" is involved in a task, students often seek out numbers they can multiply—as they believe they are supposed to do. "Area equals formula use" seems to be the unspoken assumption. This assumption works well in many tasks that involve area but not necessarily the areas of irregular figures like this triangle.

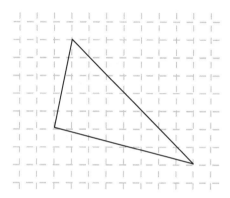

For this figure, finding the exact area requires considerable reasoning—e.g., thinking about the relationships between this triangle and the geometric figures defined by the underlying grid, perhaps leading to reasoning how one might use knowledge of areas of more regular figures (like a surrounding rectangle or composite interior triangles as shown here) to calculate the area of this irregular figure.

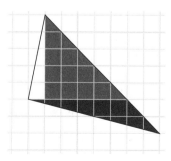

In our experience, without these reasoning options in their repertoires, many students make incorrect assumptions (such as, the angle on the lower left is a right angle), and they estimate side lengths (such as, the base side is

8 units and the height is 5 units). From there, they believe they can calculate area using the formula $^{b}h/_2$ (in this case, resulting in 20 square units, which is smaller than the actual area of 21 square units).

## Quantitative Reasoning

From the Common Core Standards of Mathematical Practice (SMP) descriptions of mathematical practices, specifically Mathematical Practice 2, *Reason abstractly and quantitatively*: "Quantitative reasoning entails habits of creating a coherent representation of the problem at hand; considering the units involved; attending to the meaning of quantities, not just how to compute them." In addition, quantitative reasoning involves "reasoning about the relationships among (quantities) without support of variable assignments or algebraic expressions" (99).[7]

Just as we want to emphasize spatial/geometric properties and relationships, as well as the language used to describe them, we also want to emphasize quantities and quantitative relationships and the language used to describe them. Much of early- and middle-grades mathematics is about quantities and relationships among quantities, but in our view, too often reasoning with and about quantities and relationships takes a back seat to applying computational procedures without much reasoning.

Another aspect of quantitative reasoning cited in the Common Core State Standards (CCSS) Mathematical Practices description is the ability to decontextualize and contextualize when using mathematics to solve problems. For example, suppose a word problem says that *Maria has $10 more than Albert, and together they have $40*. We can write a symbolic representation of this situation, say, $M + A = (A + 10) + A = 40$, with M and A representing, respectively, Maria's amount and Albert's amount. In doing so, we have *decontextualized* the situation, that is, abstracted the quantitative information from the situation. When we pause to check back in the problem, to see if we should be substituting $A + 10$ for M (as opposed, say, to something else, like $A - 10$), we have *contextualized*—gone back to the context to see if we are representing the situation appropriately. And this does not apply only to symbolic representations. Suppose we drew a diagram to represent the situation, to help thinking:

---

[7]  J. Smith and P. W. Thompson, "Quantitative Reasoning and the Development of Algebraic Reasoning," in *Algebra in the Early Grades*, eds. J. Kaput, D. Carraher, and M. Blanton (New York: Erlbaum, 2007), 95–132.

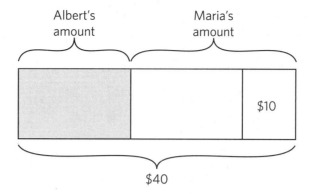

This, too, is an occasion for decontextualizing and contextualizing as the solver determines if this visual representation is an accurate portrayal of the situation described.

More generally, visual representations present a powerful tool for supporting the use of these different forms of reasoning. Here are some examples.

## Visual Representations in Quantitative Reasoning and Problem Solving

Just as geometric pictures can be used to help students—especially ELs—become more adept at noticing, reasoning about, and describing properties and relationships, so too can diagrams be useful for noticing, reasoning about, and describing quantities and relationships between them. Diagrams are a bridge between the words of tasks and their solutions, helping students by linking the relationships between quantities in the problem with the mathematical operations needed to solve the problem.

Further, diagrams can provide teachers a wonderful vehicle for prompting students to notice relationships between quantities. Read the Sharing Candies problem below, and then work to solve it. If your inclination is to solve it without diagrams, do so, and then go back and try it with diagramming:

| **Sharing Candies** |
| --- |

Sara had a bag of candies. She gave $\frac{1}{3}$ of the candies to Raul. Then Sara gave $\frac{1}{4}$ of the candies she had left to Jasmine.

After giving candies to Raul and Jasmine, Sara had 24 candies left in her bag. How many candies did Sara have at the beginning?

**Create a diagram that helps you to solve the problem. Show your work.**

In one classroom, the teacher had student groups (including ELs) present their solutions. Here is an example of the diagrams that students created and shared:

This example is color coded—in this case the rectangle on the left in black and the square in the bottom middle in gray—so not only are the amounts of candy given to Raul and Jasmine displayed clearly but so is the quantitative relationship between the two (Jasmine's amount was half of Raul's). Furthermore, an EL student presenting about a diagram like this one said, "We could see from this that Sara gave away the same number that she kept," to which one student from another group exclaimed, "I didn't see that!" Since Sara kept twenty-four, that meant she had started with forty-eight candies. This demonstrated that diagrams occasionally can reveal relationships that may not be apparent in totally symbolic approaches to the tasks.

Using diagrams is valuable in that the diagrams can, with minimal use of words, tell a story about how thinking has progressed during problem solving, and these stories can reveal EL student thinking to teachers in ways that words may not. Here is an example of a type of diagram we saw in EL student work on Sharing Candies:

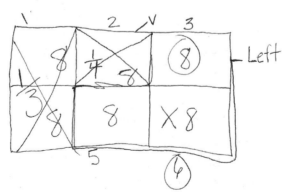

A narrative unfolds from a diagram such as this one that may go beyond the few phrases an EL might write. The story told by this diagram can be verbalized as: *First, divide a rectangle into 3 parts and denote one of the parts as "$1/3$"; then divide the remaining part of the rectangle into 4 parts and denote one part as "$1/4$." The other 3 parts are what is "left," so draw an outline around them. Go back and divide the "$1/3$" part into 2 equal parts. Now the original rectangle is divided into 6 equal parts. 3 of those parts total 24, which is what Sara had left, so each small part represents 8 pieces of candy. With 8 pieces in each of the 6 parts of the original rectangle, that says that the total amount Sara started with is **48 pieces of candy**.*

## Visual Representations in Analytic Reasoning

Because the use of mathematical visual representations *as thinking tools* is foreign to most of our middle graders, we faced a steep uphill struggle to make them part of the fabric of mathematics learning for ELs. We began to see that analytic reasoning was a critical piece in solving this puzzle. By helping students become more adept at analyzing visual representations, we reasoned, teachers would be fostering students' own use of visual representations as thinking and problem-solving tools. This can occur when teachers ask students to present their methods of solution to the rest of the class, with visual records of their thinking, such as diagrams, on the board, screen, or chart paper. Teachers can stimulate analysis by asking pointed questions, such as "Where in that diagram do you see the $1/4$ of what Sara had left?"

In addition to these exercises in analyzing each other's thinking and solving, students can analyze fictional students' use of visual representations as tools for solving problems. This is a variation on so-called *worked examples*, a research-based strategy that has proven fruitful in teaching problem-solving strategies.[8] For example, students might be shown the Sharing Candies problem (assuming they'd not seen it before), then shown the work of a student named Janet, one step at a time. In pairs, as the steps are revealed, they write answers to prompts such as: "What changed from step 1 to step 2?" "What changed from step 2 to step 3?" and so on. After the last step, each pair writes its answer to the question: "What did Janet discover?"

---

[8]  See, for example, J. L. Booth, K. E. Lange, K. R. Koedinger, and K. J. Newton, "Example Problems That Improve Student Learning in Algebra: Differentiating Between Correct and Incorrect Examples," *Learning and Instruction* 25 (2013): 24–34.

**Janet's Work on Sharing Candies**

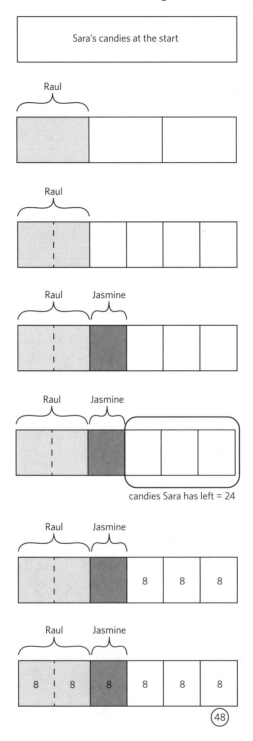

The use of worked examples in this way, combined with opportunities for students to provide mathematical explanations for those worked examples, give them a chance to engage in analytic reasoning, thinking about how those problem-solving steps help to solve the mathematics task. Of course, we do not mean that a problem-solving procedure is provided and then students copy it! Laboratory research suggests that students use novice strategies (e.g., trial and error) when presented with traditional practice exercises but employ more efficient problem-solving strategies and rely on structural aspects of problems when presented with worked examples before solving (Cooper and Sweller 1987).[9] Worked examples support problem-solving transfer by developing students' understanding of how to reach a solution and methods of problem solving (e.g., Booth et al. 2013,[10] Cooper and Sweller 1987,[9] and Sweller and Cooper 1985[11]).

We chose a variation on worked examples because they can reduce cognitive overload; students can devote less working memory to the detail of how to get to a solution and instead focus on planning their work, describing their analysis of the visual representations and making connections to other tasks (Cooper and Sweller 1987).[9] Approaches like Janet's work provide scaffolds to structure students' engagement in mathematics and language and limit the verbal- and pictorial-processing demands on working memory. We do not advocate for using only worked examples—students must have varied and frequent opportunities to create visual representations themselves for solving tasks—but we believe that using them occasionally promotes analytic reasoning by students and can be a useful tool in developing students' understanding of how to use visual representations in problem-solving contexts.

## Visual Representations in Spatial/Geometric Reasoning

The use of visual representations is perhaps most obviously connected to spatial/geometric reasoning, because geometric pictures often accompany

---

[9]  G. Cooper and J. Sweller, "Effects of Schema Acquisition and Rule Automation on Mathematical Problem-Solving Transfer," *Journal of Educational Psychology* 79, no. 4 (1987): 347–362.

[10] J. L. Booth, K. E. Lange, K. R. Koedinger, and K. J. Newton, "Example Problems That Improve Student Learning in Algebra: Differentiating Between Correct and Incorrect Examples," *Learning and Instruction* 25 (2013): 24–34.

[11] J. Sweller and G. Cooper, "The Use of Worked Examples as a Substitute for Problem Solving in Learning Algebra," *Cognition and Instruction* 2, no. 1 (1985): 59–89.

tasks. In order to foster spatial/geometric reasoning among middle graders, we have used two different strategies.

*Strategy 1.* We have engaged students, including ELs, in tasks that invite reasoning about geometric properties, in addition to those that demand reasoning about geometric measurement, such as area and perimeter. An example is:

*Parallelogram Problem*

A parallelogram has three of its vertices at the three points shown on this grid. Draw a fourth point on the grid that makes the four points the vertices of a parallelogram. Once you have found one point that works, find another. How many can you find?

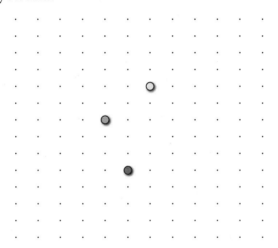

*Strategy 2.* For tasks that do involve area, perimeter, or volume measurement, where spatial/geometric reasoning is not typically used by students, we again use a worked example, by showing how fictional students have reasoned out answers to geometric measurement tasks by making use of relationships between various geometric figures. (For an example, see the Visual Representations Routine activity in Seminar 6 of the professional development materials associated with this book.) In essence, then, we employ analytic reasoning tasks to open the door to spatial/geometric reasoning.

## The Standards for Mathematical Practice

We separate out these different categories of mathematical reasoning to underscore the connections with the Common Core Standards of Mathematical

Practice (SMP). The SMP describe the mathematical thinking, or habits of mind, in which proficient doers of mathematics engage. The SMP are essential for all students, and we must therefore work to provide access to the SMP for ELs. By working on supports for problem solving and analytic reasoning, in contexts that promote spatial/geometric reasoning and quantitative reasoning, we are able to engage ELs and other students in the SMP. Problem solving is addressed directly in SMP 1 (*Make sense of problems and persevere in solving them*), while analytic reasoning is essential to SMP 3 (*Construct viable arguments and critique the reasoning of others*). When working with visual representations in contexts that support quantitative reasoning, SMP 2 (*Reason abstractly and quantitatively*) is a natural fit because mathematical diagrams aid in moving back and forth between the quantities, their relationships, and what they represent. Spatial/geometric reasoning contexts can propel SMP 7 (*Look for and make use of structure*) because the geometric structure (e.g., the relationships between different geometric figures or components of those figures) become important. Furthermore, we emphasize explicit language strategies and the use of visual representations in part because they elicit, respectively, SMP 6 (*Attend to precision*) and SMP 5 (*Use appropriate tools strategically*).

We will discuss more about the Standards for Mathematical Practice and how they relate to the work of ELs in Chapters 3 and 4.

## A Design Framework for Creating Access

The following four ingredients constitute our design framework for creating access for ELs:

- Challenging mathematical tasks
- Multimodal representation
- Development of mathematical communication
- Repeated structured practice

A critical feature underlying this design framework is the belief that, in order for mathematics teachers to help the ELs in their classes, they should regularly integrate academic language development with visual representations to open access to challenging mathematical tasks. Instructional routines—an enactment of repeated structured practices—structure and power this integration. These four key ingredients must be used in concert to be most successful. In this book we will focus in on each ingredient in at least one chapter; below, we give a short introduction to each.

## Challenging Tasks

Teachers regularly include challenging mathematics tasks in instruction of their students of all English language proficiency levels. We gauge the degree of challenge in mathematics tasks by how much they engage students in various combinations of problem solving, analytic reasoning, spatial/geometric reasoning, and quantitative reasoning.

Generally and informally, "productive struggle" in mathematics means doing genuine mathematical work, such as engaging in problem solving and other kinds of mathematical reasoning. Tasks induce productive struggle to the extent that the questions "Is real mathematical work being done?" and "Who is doing it?" can be answered as "The *students* are doing the mathematical work on the task, and it is work in which they need to reason, or conjecture, or make a viable argument, and so on."

We will address this topic in detail in Chapter 5. For now, it suffices to say that this principle is based on a strong foundation, namely, the findings in the QUASAR study of urban middle-school mathematics classrooms, which showed that a regular diet of mathematics tasks with high cognitive demand improves student performance across the student population, including EL students.[12]

## Multimodal Representations

Teachers use and promote multiple modes for expressing mathematical reasoning with their students of all English proficiency levels. In particular, they use, and help ELs use, mathematical visual representations. Classroom environments making ample use of multiple modes—pictures, diagrams, presentations, written explanations, and gestures—afford ELs the means first to understand the mathematics they are engaged with, and second to express the thinking behind their reasoning and problem solving. We will discuss multimodal representations, particularly visual representations, further in Chapter 2, but for now we want to emphasize that engaging students through a variety of modes, especially the nonverbal, like gestures and

---

[12] M. Henningsen and M. K. Stein, "Mathematical Tasks and Student Cognition: Classroom-Based Factors That Support and Inhibit High-Level Mathematical Thinking and Reasoning," *Journal for Research in Mathematics Education* 28, no. 5 (1997): 524–49.

mathematical visual representations, can provide non-English speakers the access and engagement that they need to succeed in mathematics.

## Development of Mathematical Communication

Mathematics teachers help their students of all English proficiency levels develop the ability to communicate (by reading, writing, speaking, and listening) about mathematics. This includes both informal language used to explain mathematical thinking and the development of academic language, which are developed by *using* both informal and academic language to talk about mathematics. Teachers can do so by employing language access and language-production strategies that are integrated with the mathematical goals of lessons.

For one example: In the original version of the Sharing Candies problem, we feared the context (children sharing marbles on the playground), and possibly the wording, might be unfamiliar to students from other cultures, and we worked to make the context and language accessible to ELs. Even after those revisions (which resulted in the task you see), we were concerned about accessibility, so we wove a language access strategy into the implementation of the task, called the "Three Reads" strategy:

| Sharing Candies |
|---|

Sara had a bag of candies.  She gave $\frac{1}{3}$ of the candies to Raul.
Then Sara gave $\frac{1}{4}$ of the candies she had left to Jasmine.

After giving candies to Raul and Jasmine, Sara had 24 candies left in her bag.  How many candies did Sara have at the beginning?

**Create a diagram that helps you to solve the problem.  Show your work.**

| 1ˢᵗ Read | **CONTEXT**<br><br>The problem is about _____. |
|---|---|
| 2ⁿᵈ Read | **PURPOSE**<br><br>I need to _____. |
| 3ʳᵈ Read | **INFORMATION**<br>• <br><br>• |

In employing this strategy, the teacher leads the students through three readings of the problem, each time having them write down their answers to a different question: "What is the problem about?" (e.g., candy, or sharing candy, or sharing candies with two friends, and so on); "What is the problem asking you to find?" (how many candies Sara had in the beginning); and "What is some important information given?" (E.g., she gave $1/3$ to Raul; she gave $1/4$ of what's left to Jasmine; 24 left in the bag). This strategy came to mind because EL specialists advise teachers to "slow things down" when access by ELs is at risk—as with the risk of cognitive overload presented by a word problem. The Three Reads strategy operationalizes the advice to slow things down. Teachers and students—including native English speakers—appear to like it. In fact, one student in the class of one of our collaborating teachers asked his teacher if he "could use Three Reads on the MCAS" (the Massachusetts state examination). (See Chapter 4 for more information about the Three Reads and other language access instructional strategies.)

## Repeated Structured Practices

Teachers engage students of all English proficiency levels in instructional routines designed to help the teacher focus on the use of challenging mathematical tasks, multimodal representation, and development of academic language.

Routinizing—that is to say, repeatedly using the same instructional sequence—allows teachers to focus more on their students and the mathematical content with which their students are grappling. Both teachers and students become familiar with the steps of the routine and do not need to spend as much cognitive effort on the mechanics of enacting the routine. Teachers can instead focus on how particular strategies support particular students (e.g., students who are ELs) and what their students are learning. They can take opportunities to "tinker" with the strategies embedded in the routine to learn what works best for students. In this manner, using mathematical instructional routines contributes to building teacher capacity for meeting students' needs.

Our use of the term "instructional routine" is drawn from a growing literature on "well-designed procedures that have been proven in practice, that take account of the complexity of the goals that need to be accomplished, and that allow the practitioner temporarily to hold some things constant while working on others (130)."[13] Instructional procedures are intended to help teachers manage complexity in instruction, such as adapting to what they observe in students' work during lessons. In mathematics, they are generally designed to provide opportunities for students to reason about mathematical ideas.

We will discuss routines further in Chapter 6.

## Summary

In our work with mathematics teachers with students who are ELs, all of our efforts are based on a commitment to *access* for ELs to opportunities for productive engagement with mathematics.

You may have heard a sentiment we have heard, namely, that in meeting the challenges in ensuring ELs' success in mathematics, "mathematics teachers must be language teachers as well." There is truth to the statement, but that particular framing makes it sound as if teachers of mathematics must sign up for an additional career. Rather, we prefer to argue that mathematics teachers need not veer from their chosen profession. We deeply believe that our four principles, which undergird this entire book, can make it possible to foster mathematics success for ELs from within the *learning and doing of mathematics*.

Even with our arguments and examples, the four design principles may still seem abstract, so we close this chapter with quotes from two teachers who worked with us, as they looked back at what they had learned and what they noted about ELs in their classes:

> [S]eeing the different ways that they [the students] can use diagrams, just even having that idea of a diagram in their head and maybe having a couple of different pictures of what could be a diagram; [. . . it] can help them to then sometimes use it as a strategy anytime they are getting stuck.

---

[13] M. Lampert, H. Beasley, H. Ghousseini, E. Kazemi, and M. Franke, "Using Designed Instructional Activities to Enable Novices to Manage Ambitious Mathematics Teaching," in *Instructional Explanations in the Disciplines*, eds. M. K. Stein and L. Kucan (Springer Science+Business Media, LLC, 2010).

> As time progressed, they understood the value of it (diagramming). They recognized that it was a math tool and not an art project. And they got really excited when they explained someone else's diagram. And that is where it registered for me that they understood what they were doing.

In the next chapter, we explore more deeply the use of mathematical visual representations to create greater access for English learners to mathematical thinking and mathematical communication.

# Chapter 2

# Why Visual Representations?

How would you think about the following word problem, if you set out to solve it?

*Roberto spent ²/₅ of his money on computer games. He spent $20 on those games. How much money did Roberto have before he bought the games?*

Word problems like this one are described as algebraic because they ask solvers to work backward from given information to a starting point (e.g., how much money Roberto had at the start). A very common way to approach such problems is to:

1. "Let *x* equal" the quantity we are trying to find.

2. Use the given information to construct an equation.

3. Solve for the value of *x* in the equation.

In the present case, *x* could equal the amount of money Roberto had at the start, and then a relevant equation is $(^2/_5)x = 20$. From there, solving for the value of *x* requires a level of calculating proficiency that may be beyond many elementary school students, perhaps even middle school students.

However, the very same students could succeed with more visual, less computational ways of representing algebraic word problems.[1] For example, an approach using tape diagrams (sometimes called strip diagrams) might point to a solution with the following sequence of representations:

1.

2. money spent = ²⁄₅

3. money spent = $20

4.                          money left = ³⁄₅

5. money spent = $20          money left = $30

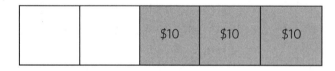

[1] S. Beckmann, "Solving Algebra and Other Story Problems with Simple Diagrams: A Method Demonstrated in Grade 4–6 Texts Used in Singapore," *The Mathematics Educator* 14, no. 1 (2004): 42–46.

From there, it should be a quick step, adding the five $10s, to figure that Roberto had $50 to start with, which is the sought-after information in the task.

We are especially interested in such visual tools for their potential value for students who are English learners (ELs). As we described in the previous chapter, multimodal representation, along with challenging mathematical tasks, developing mathematical communication, and repeated structured practices, is a key design principle of our work with ELs. In this chapter and the next, we look more deeply at the roles of multimodal representation in creating access, especially the essential and multipurpose contributions of mathematical visual representations. Those contributions are both cognitive and pedagogical, that is, there are ways in which visual representations benefit the learners themselves directly, and there are ways in which they benefit learners indirectly, through the instructional affordances they offer teachers. For example, a student represents a geometric transformation of a triangle with a curved arrow. The teacher might ask: "What happened to the triangle here?" The student might make a gesture suggesting a rotation, after which the teacher could say, "I think you mean you imagined you rotated the triangle, right? That's called a rotation." Or, a teacher might help a student be more analytical about her own diagram: "Where in your diagram is the total of Sonia's money? Where is the $1/4$ of her money she gave to Tomas?"

All students are capable of mathematical thinking even when they are not skilled at verbally expressing their ideas. Moschkovich (2002)[2] notes that, in order to develop conceptual understanding, instruction for ELs should provide opportunities to discuss mathematical concepts. She makes the case that, rather than emphasizing low-level language skills (e.g., vocabulary, pronunciation), instruction should focus on both mathematical thinking and language development. One way to focus on students' thinking while they develop proficiency in verbalizing their ideas is through the use of multimodal mathematical communication.

---

[2] J. Moschkovich, "A Situated and Sociocultural Perspective on Bilingual Mathematics Learners," *Mathematical Thinking & Learning* 4, nos. 2 and 3 (2002): 189–212.

# Multimodal Mathematical Communication— The Role of Visual Representations

Multimodal mathematical communication refers to the various ways in which students convey their mathematical thinking, including language, gestures, drawings, or the use of tools (e.g., physical models, manipulatives, and technology). Students may use a combination of modes at once or different ones in isolation. To enhance mathematical learning opportunities for all students, particularly ELs and those struggling with language, research stresses the importance of creating classroom environments that encourage multimodal communication (Chval and Khisty 2001,[3] Khisty and Chval 2002,[4] Moschkovich 2002[5]). Such environments can foster the development of the CCSS Standards for Mathematical Practice by providing students access to the mathematics, helping them construct viable arguments, and providing opportunities to attend to precision by developing accurate mathematical language.

A critical piece in fostering a culture of multimodal communication in the classroom is for teachers to value and encourage the use of mathematical visual representations such as diagrams or geometric drawings, especially as tools for reasoning and communicating mathematical thinking. Opportunities to use mathematical visual representations provide students access to mathematics, support their engagement in problem solving, facilitate communication of their mathematical thinking, and develop the mathematical practices outlined in the Common Core State Standards. Embedding such opportunities in classroom environments where teachers strive to notice evidence of students' thinking, and build on that evidence to create equity in mathematics instruction, maximizes their value. (We will discuss noticing evidence of students' thinking more in the next chapter.)

## Advantages of Visual Representation

Engagement with visual representations differs somewhat, depending on mathematical topic area.

---

[3] K. Chval and L. Khisty, *Writing in Mathematics with Latino Students*, presentation at the Annual Meeting of the American Educational Research Association, Seattle, WA (2001, April).

[4] L. L. Khisty and K. B. Chval, "Pedagogic Discourse and Equity in Mathematics: When Teachers' Talk Matters," *Mathematics Education Research Journal*, 14, no. 3 (2002): 154–68.

[5] J. Moschkovich, "A Situated and Sociocultural Perspective on Bilingual Mathematics Learners."

## Spatial/Geometric Reasoning

In geometry, many tasks are presented with accompanying drawings. In such cases, solvers may advance their thinking by experimenting with the drawings—for example, by adding auxiliary lines within or between given figures. Consider how a student, Mario, approached the transformation of a triangle into a rectangle in order to find the area of the triangle:

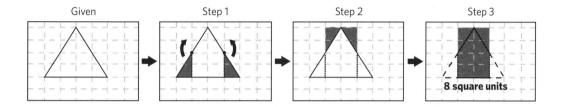

The lines Mario used to cut and move pieces around are examples of "auxiliary lines" (lines, rays, or line segments added to a geometric figure to help in solving a problem or constructing a proof). This kind of engagement with geometric representations is consistent with Common Core Mathematical Practice 7: *Looking for and making use of structure.*

When presented with a geometric reasoning task, many students will bypass the invitation to reason and rush to apply a formula—often inappropriately. In the process, they often ignore the geometric figures they are presented with and how the figures themselves are tools to help solve the task. For example, consider the following task:

*Find two different methods for calculating the area of the following figure:*

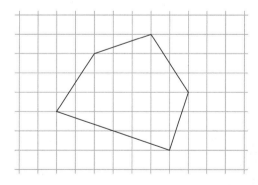

As you look at this irregular pentagon, sitting on a grid, where might you draw auxiliary lines to help you calculate? One option is to look outside the figure. That could lead to creating and calculating the area of a 7 by 6

rectangle and subtracting from it the areas of the outside figures: five right triangles and the one little rectangle.

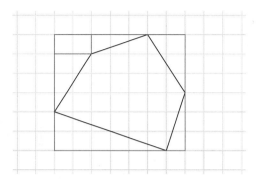

Another option is to stay inside the figure, for example, finding friendly triangles and rectangles as in this combination:

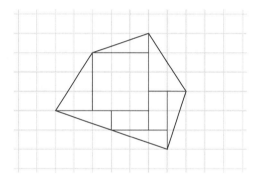

It is also possible to use Mario's strategy on this pentagon, that is, to dissect the pentagon and reconfigure the pieces as a friendlier figure (below). You can see how the problem solvers denoted the cuts and rotations of pieces. By performing these transformations, they managed to turn the pentagon into a 5 by 5 square. From there, calculating the area is straightforward: 25 square units.

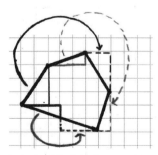

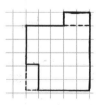

5 × 5

This kind of task stops many students cold, because they know only *one* way to calculate area—that is, to use a formula involving the measures of the figure's sides and altitudes. It is a trained procedure—a good shortcut at times but not a substitute for understanding the concept of area. Nor is it a good substitute for activating and using Mathematical Practice 7, *Look for and make use of structure*. Seeing structure in a geometric situation, and not just numbers to compute with, is very important in the development of mathematical thinking. Using visual representations, specifically geometric drawings, can support students in seeing structure in a geometric situation and in their geometric problem solving more generally. In this task, visual representation comes into play by expanding a given representation, thus opening the door for finding different ways to calculate the area for this irregular pentagon.

Making use of visual representations as geometric reasoning tools extends well beyond area tasks, even in middle grades. For example, a typical structural feature in geometry is a *line of symmetry*. If there appears to be an invisible line of symmetry, drawing that line as an auxiliary line can make features apparent that were not apparent before. For middle graders adept at paper-folding tasks, lines of symmetry often appear as a result of a fold, which represents a line of reflection. With practice, one usually can envision and draw the auxiliary symmetry lines without having to fold the paper.

A classic example is the task of showing that a triangle with two congruent sides—that is, an isosceles triangle—has two congruent angles.

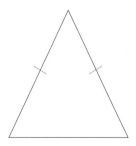

A natural candidate for line of symmetry here is the segment from the top vertex and bisecting the base:

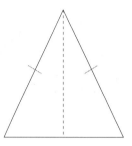

A middle grader might try "folding it in half," that is, imagining a segment running from the peak of the triangle to the middle of the base and using this imagined segment as a fold line. Looking at the results of the fold, the student might realize "Hey, everything fits together. The angles match!" Without actually folding paper, students might *imagine* the folding happening and come to the same conclusion.

Students with more geometry in their background might go further in using the auxiliary line and reason through to a viable argument (Mathematical Practice 3) by thinking, "Okay, the line does look like a line of symmetry. There are two right triangles, and each looks like the reflection of the other through the line of symmetry. Each of the three pairs of corresponding sides is a congruent pair. So, the two triangles are congruent to each other, by side-side-side. They *are* reflections of each other. So, the two base angles of the isosceles triangle are congruent."

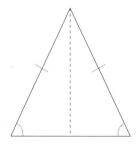

(As a side note: In arguing this way, the student would be true to CCSS Standard G-CO-6: *Use geometric descriptions of rigid motions to transform figures and to predict the effect of a given rigid motion on a given figure; given two figures, use the definition of congruence in terms of rigid motions to decide if they are congruent.*)

Evidently, geometric drawings can support students' mathematical thinking in many ways. They provide students with a variety of entry points for considering geometric ideas in ways that support their productive struggle. When we talk about supporting ELs with the use of visual representations, geometric drawings are, therefore, an important piece of this recommendation.

## Quantitative Reasoning

Unlike geometry tasks, tasks in middle-grade mathematics where quantitative reasoning is prominent, such as in algebra word problems, usually do *not* provide visual representations. In such cases, knowing how to draw one's own visual representations, in the form of diagrams, is a very valuable skill—especially for ELs. To solve a written mathematics problem, a student has to read the text of the problem, make sense of the text, particularly the numerical and spatial relationships presented, and eventually represent the information in arithmetical expressions and equations. Diagrams can provide a bridge from text to arithmetical representations. To be able to do this readily, a student needs to develop *diagram sense*—knowing when various visual representations are most useful—for example, knowing that tree diagrams can help organize probabilistic thinking; that number lines are often handy for rational-number tasks; and that tape diagrams can propel thinking about algebraic word problems. We know that students need to develop *number sense* in order to judge the reasonableness in their own and others' calculations. We also know that number sense can be learned through ample opportunities to reason about numbers and operations. Similarly, we believe that *diagram sense* can be learned through ample opportunities to represent problems and to reason with the diagrams.

Mathematical diagrams, like geometric drawings, are important visual representations to support and promote mathematical thinking for all students. Mathematical representations of problems should provide opportunities to use the representation to make sense of the problem, make modifications in light of sense making, and select a solution strategy (Ng and Lee 2008).[6] Eventually, we want students to acquire and use the various forms of algebraic representations, but it is possible to build toward them and to do so in ways that elicit mathematical practices (as we will see more in the next chapter). Creating and analyzing a diagram is a powerful tool in that service. A diagram can call students' attention to the quantities presented in a problem, along with the relationships between quantities. The 2012 IES Practice Guide, *Improving Mathematical Problem Solving in Grades 4–8,*[7] which is based on an examination of hundreds of relevant, rigorous studies, identified five recommendations, the third of which is to teach students how to use visual representations: "Students who learn to visually represent the mathematical information in problems prior to writing an equation are more effective at problem solving" (Woodward et al. 2012, 23). Visual representations, such as number lines, tape diagrams, and drawings "help scaffold learning and pave the way for understanding the abstract version of the representation" (Gersten et al. 2009, 31).[8]

For example, in the sequence of diagrams used earlier for the Roberto problem, the solver would need to keep track of the given quantities, $2/5$ (of the unknown amount of money) and $20, as well as become aware of the related quantities $3/5$ and $60. The tape diagram can help the solver manage this information. Diagrams can help students understand relationships among quantities, sometimes even hidden relationships that the words and numbers used to solve the problem may otherwise obscure. Consider the Sharing Candies problem from Chapter 1:

> *Sara had a bag of candies. She gave $1/3$ of the candies to Raul. Then Sara gave $1/4$ of the candies she had left to Jasmine. After giving candies to Raul*

[6] S. F. Ng and K. Lee, "The Model Method: Singapore Children's Tool for Representing and Solving Algebraic Word Problems," *Journal for Research in Mathematics Education* 40, no. 3 (2009): 282–313.

[7] J. Woodward et al., *Improving Mathematical Problem Solving in Grades 4 Through 8: A Practice Guide* (NCEE 2012-4055) (Washington, DC: National Center for Education Evaluation and Regional Assistance, Institute of Education Sciences, U.S. Department of Education, 2012). Retrieved from http://ies.ed.gov/ncee/wwc/publications_reviews.aspx#pubsearch/.
M. Larson and M. Driscoll, *Addressing the Achievement Gap in Mathematics Through Improved Problem Solving: Webinar* (2013). Retrieved from http://www.relcentral.org/events/past-events/.

[8] R. Gersten, S. Beckmann, B. Clarke, A. Foegen, L. Marsh, J. R. Star, and B. Witzel, *Assisting Students Struggling with Mathematics: Response to Intervention (RtI) for Elementary and Middle Schools* (NCEE 2009-4060). (Washington, DC: National Center for Education Evaluation and Regional Assistance, Institute of Education Sciences, U.S. Department of Education, 2009). Retrieved from http://ies.ed.gov/ncee/wwc/publications/practiceguides/.

*and Jasmine, Sara had 24 candies left in her bag. How many candies did Sara have at the beginning?*

Recall the example diagram from Chapter 1, shown in the figure below:

One small group of students presenting about a similar diagram included a descriptive key that read "Blue shows $^1/_3$ of Sara's candies; green shows $^1/_4$ of what was left." (The rectangle on the left was shaded blue and the rectangle in the bottom middle was shaded green.) As described in Chapter 1, an EL presenting the diagram said, "We could see from this that Sara gave away the same number that she kept," to which one student from another group exclaimed, "I didn't see that!" Because Sara kept 24, that meant she had started with 48 candies.

Two things stand out about this incident. First, the "gave away as much as she kept" relationship might have remained hidden to the students, like the student who shouted, if they were just trying to crank out a symbolic, algebraic approach to set up the situation. This demonstrated that diagrams occasionally can reveal relationships that may not be apparent in totally symbolic approaches to the tasks. Second, the picture makes clear that there is nothing special about the number 24, that is, the relationship remains no matter how many candies Sara started with—a bit of algebra without the symbols.

Tape and grid diagrams are not the only helpful diagrams. Consider the following algebraic word problem:

*It used to take Miguel $^2/_3$ of an hour to drive to his office. Last month, his company moved six miles farther away from his home. It now takes Miguel $^5/_6$ of an hour to drive to his office at the same speed. How far away from his office does Miguel live?*

Before considering a visual representation, think in the way many of us were taught to approach this problem: "Let $x$ equal . . . what?" If you reach an answer this way, now consider a visual approach. Try to think of something other than a tape or grid diagram. What other representations come to mind?

One option might be a double number line:

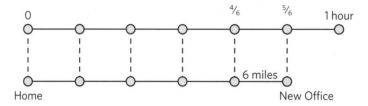

The diagram captures the quantitative chunks of information in the problem: the distance to the old office; the time it took to get to the old office; the increase of distance to the new office; and the time it takes to get to the new office. One more step can help: Divide the time into equal-sized intervals, and match them with equal-sized intervals in the distance. As in many of these problems, we make assumptions, which in this case include the assumption that Miguel travels at a constant rate. Note how the diagram itself makes this assumption transparently clear: The intervals on the bottom line are uniformly the same size, corresponding to the same-sized time intervals above.

Once again, the relationships between quantities are revealed, and so are possible pathways to a solution. For example: $1/6$ of an hour is equivalent to six miles; $5/6$ of an hour is equivalent to thirty miles. Miguel now has a thirty-mile commute.

## Diagrams vs. Pictures

When confronted by problems like those above, all students—especially students who are learning English—should learn to employ a habit of mind that asks "Can I draw something helpful here?" The word *helpful* is critical. In talking about visual images as a thinking tool, it is important to distinguish between *pictorial imagery* and *schematic imagery*. The former refers to constructing detailed visual images—for example, in the Sharing Candies problem, it might be a drawing of Sara handing out candies from a bag. Very often, these narrative depictions have context-decoding value but no mathematical value. Thus, a picture might explain the context of the task, possibly valuable information to English learners, but contain very little mathematical information with which to solve it.

*Schematic imagery* refers to the mathematical visual representations as addressed in this book: representations of geometric and quantitative relationships between objects. This might involve diagramming and drawing auxiliary lines, or transforming geometric figures, say by imagining cutting pieces of a figure and rotating them in order to line them up in a convenient way. Research has shown that "use of schematic representations is positively related to success in mathematical problem solving, whereas use of pictorial representations is negatively related to success in mathematical problem solving" (Hegarty and Kozhevnikov 1999, 688).[9]

# Visual Representations and Access for EL Students

Whether in lessons or on tests, multistep word problems present special challenges for English learners, who must work out the meanings being conveyed by the words, then translate those meanings into a solution strategy that, in turn, is translated into mathematical processes and abstract symbols. In such cases, mathematical diagrams can act as a bridge of access between words and symbols.

Consider the challenges to reasoning in the following word problem:

---

### How Many People?

The population of the town of Medtown is three times the size of the population of the town of Carburg.
The *difference* in the number of people in the two towns is 2,184 people.
How many people live in Medtown and Carburg **combined**?
Create a diagram that helps you to solve the problem. Show your work.

---

This can be a tricky problem to set up for any student. Four quantities and three operations are referred to (the quantities are the two populations, their difference, and their combined number; the operations are multiplication, subtraction, and addition). It is possible, though not necessarily easy, to set this up and solve it algebraically. (If $M$ represents the population of Medtown and $C$ the population of Carburg, students often cannot decide

---

[9] M. Hegarty and M. Kozhevnikov, "Types of Visual-Spatial Representations and Mathematical Problem Solving," *Journal of Educational Psychology* 91, no. 4 (1999): 684–89.

whether the correct equation from the first sentence of the task is 3M = C or 3C = M.)[10] Arguably, diagramming the task is a better way to lay out the quantities and the computational relationships among the quantities. Something like the following is possible—and we have seen similar from students and teachers—using tape diagrams (and colors or shading) to represent the various quantities and relationships:

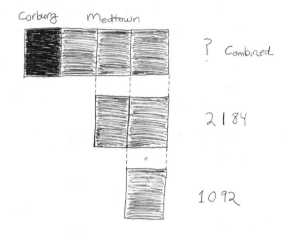

Here is an alternative type of representation, using a number line combined with strips:

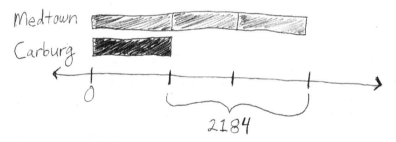

In the first, the area of the Medtown rectangle is three times the area of the Carburg rectangle. Similarly, in the second representation, the length of the Medtown segment is three times the length of the Carburg segment. In the representations, the quantities of area and length substitute for the population quantity. In each case, the representation could very well reveal the meaning of the first sentence of the task more clearly, without the potential confusion in deciding between 3M = C or 3C = M.

---

[10] J. Clement, "Algebra Word Problem Solutions: Thought Processes Underlying a Common Misconception," *Journal for Research in Mathematics Education*, 13, no. 1 (1982): 16–30.

Such a visual bridge between the verbal presentation and symbolic representation of a task can be particularly helpful to English learners in accessing the meaning of the task. While all students benefit from understanding and creating visual representations of mathematics tasks, the benefit appears particularly important for English learners. In tackling word problems in English, English learners must decode the meaning of the language, which is fraught with challenges, particularly when contextual vocabulary, use of complex clauses, and other linguistic hurdles are present. In our work involving ELs, we have found that creating and using diagrams in mathematical problem solving can provide an important bridge. Visual representations can link the verbal representation that sets out the task with the symbolic representations that push toward solution.

A study of Singapore students' use of diagrams described this bridging from verbal representation to abstract representation by pointing out that abstract representation of a task divides "into two specific phases, the structural phase and the procedural-symbolic phase, with the nature of each phase clearly specified" (Ng and Lee 2009, 291).[11] The drawing reveals structural features like "the inputs, the relationships between the inputs, and the output of the problem" (291). These can reveal themselves in the diagram without reliance on numbers and other symbols. For example, for the structural phase, both of the above diagrams for the How Many People? task reveal, without recourse to any symbolism, the inputs (the unknown populations are drawn; and the difference between the populations is recognizable as a rectangle and a line segment, even without the 2184 label); relationships between inputs (the 3:1 ratio of populations shows up, as does the relationship that the difference of populations is twice the size of the smaller population); and the output of the problem (the output, the combination of the two populations, shows up clearly as four times the smaller population or two times the difference). Once all these structural elements are recognized, the solver can proceed to the procedural-symbolic phase, putting together procedures with numbers and other symbols to represent what the structural elements reveal about the output. In this case, it might be something like: "$C + M = 2 \times$ Difference or $2 \times (M - C)$ or $2 \times 2184$ or $4368$." We believe it is this capacity of diagrams to separate task structure from symbols

---

[11] S. F. Ng and K. Lee, "The Model Method: Singapore Children's Tool for Representing and Solving Algebraic Word Problems," *Journal for Research in Mathematics Education* 40, no. 3 (2009): 282–313.

and procedures that effectively creates the bridge from verbal representation of a task to symbolic representation and so enhances access for EL students.

There are other benefits for ELs, and indeed for other students as well, in the regular use of visual representations. For instance, there are ways to exploit diagrams to ease transition to algebraic approaches to word problems. Color is one such way. Everything related to Medtown in the How Many People? task might be in red, say, and everything related to Carburg might be in blue—both the visual representations and the algebraic representations using *M* and *C*. In that way, color maps algebraic use of letters back to diagrammatic representations of a task's structural elements. Sometimes students will use colors in this way, and the teacher can point out the correspondence to the entire class. In other instances, teachers can do the color correspondences themselves. ELs can benefit in other, indirect ways from regular use of visual representations. An EL's visual representation can reveal much about the student's mathematical thinking, which he or she may not have the words to express. Attending to this evidence of thinking provides invaluable data for teachers to work with. Another benefit arises from the EL's linguistic engagement with a diagram, naming and then describing features of a diagram, and eventually using the features to explain and make viable mathematical arguments. These benefits open the door for the mathematics teacher to understand the student's reasoning and use of language and then to help the student improve them.

## Purposes for Visual Representations

In our work, we have been struck by a common misapprehension about visual representations, and diagrams in particular, both by students and teachers—namely, that the primary purpose of a diagram is to present the *product* of one's thinking about a mathematical task. Other mathematics educators[12] have noted similar findings. No doubt this is a helpful role for diagrams, but it is far from the only, or even most valuable, purpose of diagramming. Rather, visual representations, including diagrams and geometric drawings, can be really effective **reasoning tools** for learners trying to solve challenging mathematical tasks. And this is a quality that makes them especially valuable for ELs, as is the use of visual representations as **communication tools**. From our classroom observations and interviews

---

[12] D. A. Stylianou, "An Examination of Middle School Students' Representation Practices in Mathematical Problem Solving Through the Lens of Expert Work: Towards an Organizing Scheme," *Educational Studies in Mathematics* 76 (2011): 265–80.

of teachers and coaches, we have compiled a set of different purposes for working with visual representations in mathematics lessons. They are listed in the next table.

| Purpose: Support Mathematical Reasoning | |
| --- | --- |
| **1. Students start work on a task by representing important information from the mathematical task or context:**<br>• See/show given quantities or given geometric figures.<br>• See/show given relationships between quantities or figures.<br>• Uncover additional relationships between quantities or figures or properties of figures. | For example, in both numbers and geometry, diagrams can reveal relationships between quantities and between figures, e.g., the 3:1 relationship between the populations of Medtown to Carburg in the How Many People? task, or the relationship between the area of an irregular figure and the areas of constituent regular figures.<br>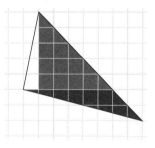 |
| **2. Students work on or think about a mathematical question:**<br>• Get started on finding a solution path for a mathematics task.<br>• Find one or more solution path(s).<br>• Solve the task.<br>• Generate additional mathematical questions. | For example, using double number lines for a percent problem can lead to thinking of percent as a rate (per 100). |
| **3. Students share a mathematical approach or mathematical thinking.**<br>• Share thinking with others (with or without using a lot of words).<br>• Articulate own thinking.<br>• Support teachers' understanding of student's thinking.<br>• Reveal relationships others may not have seen. | For example, a student might show how she revised her diagram solving a task and explain why she thought she should. |

*Continued*

| Purpose: Support Productive and Receptive Language Use | |
|---|---|
| **4. Students produce mathematical language:**<br>• Verbally describe what the diagramming shows (could be linked to any of the above purposes). | For example:<br><br>Student points at the chart paper and says, "We could see from this that Sara gave away the same number that she kept." |
| **5. Students develop understanding of a term, phrase, concept, or problem context:**<br>• Review a diagram or visual representation that shows the meaning of a term, phrase, or concept. | For example:<br>A fraction bar shows students that $1/5$ is indicated.<br>An array diagram can show why $1/4 \times 2/3$ is $1/6$. |

Despite their many affordances, visual representations by themselves cannot fulfill their promise for opening doors of access for ELs. But with teachers' purposeful use of them, they can have that kind of impact. In the next chapter, we will look at what teachers can learn by examining students' representations with an eye toward helping EL students' mathematical competence and potential for greater mathematical competence become more visible, along with their potential to become proficient mathematical communicators.

# Chapter 3

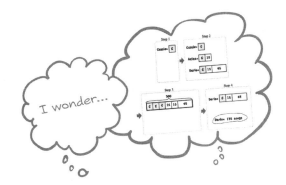

I wonder...

# Visual Representations as Evidence of Student Thinking and Potential

In 2005, while testing the *Fostering Geometric Thinking* professional development materials for middle-grade teachers,[1] we made a happy discovery, with promising implications for teaching mathematics to English learners. The materials we were testing focused mostly on geometric reasoning and analyzing student work to understand student thinking. Our participating teachers, all from a large urban district, included many teachers of ELs. The first time they brought in student work on the geometric reasoning tasks, they also brought exciting news: The teachers reported that, through analyzing their EL students' geometric drawings and gestures, it was possible to understand their thinking, even for students with low English proficiency. For the teachers, this was a welcome boost not only for understanding student thinking but also for helping students advance their geometric reasoning (e.g., through questions), as well as advance ELs' knowledge of academic

---

[1]  M. Driscoll et al., *The Fostering Geometric Thinking Toolkit: A Guide for Staff Development* (Portsmouth, NH: Heinemann, 2008).
M. Driscoll et al., *Fostering Geometric Thinking* (Portsmouth, NH: Heinemann, 2007).

language (e.g., by helping them link academic terms to features of their pictures and gestures).

As a general rule, mathematics teachers are experienced and frequently are experts in a particular kind of student-work analysis. Often forced by time constraints to examine work quickly, they are able to see who is on the right track and who is not; how many students are getting side-tracked; where students are getting side-tracked; and who might need extra instructional attention. Often, this attention is directed toward students' grasp of mathematics procedures and how to apply them.

All of this effort, in the real time of instruction, is essential to effective teaching practice. However, what often remain invisible in these hurried examinations of student work are the indications—perhaps small—of competence and potential in students' mathematical thinking. Noticing such indications can be essential in providing ELs access to mathematical proficiency.

Analyzing student work is especially informative when the tasks are mathematically challenging; when they invite visual representations of the students' work and descriptions of those representations; and when they inform and help structure teaching the next lesson.

The kind of student-work analysis that we advocate has the following five features:

1. A focus on *evidence* in the students' work. Typically, there will be evidence of mathematical thinking as well as evidence of mathematical communication. With English learners, it is important to recall that evidence of mathematical thinking is distinct from evidence of mathematical communication. Put another way, a student may be thinking productively about a mathematical task but communicating about it with difficulty.

2. In the same vein, the sweep of attention to evidence should be wide enough to take in evidence of *potential* for competence in the student's work on a task and not just evidence of deficit. Equitable instruction, we believe, is grounded in attention to both potential and needs.

3. The evidence sought in student-work analysis should be evidence of *mathematical thinking that is valued*. In past work, we have based student-work analysis on two different frameworks: an algebraic habits of mind framework when the purpose was to focus on students'

development of algebraic thinking, and a geometric habits of mind framework when the purpose was to focus on students' development of geometric thinking.[2] For a general framework of evidence of mathematical thinking, when tasks range across all of middle school mathematics, we have embraced the Common Core Standards of Mathematical Practice (SMP). Not only do they reach across the various mathematical domains, they also are intended to be the means by which the Common Core Mathematics Content Standards are put into action. Finally, we like the emphasis on *practice*, because that suggests each of the eight practices lives on a continuum, identifiable in early stages of development, as well as late.

4. For the benefit of ELs, and also for other students, the search for evidence related to *mathematical communication* should be guided by two elements: a language-development framework and the integration of language strategies with the mathematical-reasoning prompts in the tasks. Both help keep the tasks within access for most, if not all, English learners, and both are useful in managing the cognitive demands of mathematics tasks. For the language-development framework, we recommend the WIDA framework,[3] which guides EL policies and practices in many states, and which offers expectation markers for EL students at different levels of English language proficiency. Language strategies that can support students to access, develop, and produce language that you might see in their student work are described in detail in Chapter 4 as well as in examples throughout this book.

5. Finally, because we have been working with teachers of English learners, we aim to have teachers collect student work to analyze on mathematics tasks that not only elicit mathematical reasoning of the types discussed in Chapter 1 but also invite the use of *mathematical visual representations* as described in Chapters 2 and 4.

---

[2] M. Driscoll, et al., *Fostering Geometric Thinking* (Portsmouth, NH: Heinemann, 2007). M. Driscoll, *Fostering Algebraic Thinking* (Portsmouth, NH: Heinemann, 1999).

[3] WIDA, *Amplification of the English Language Development Standards, Kindergarten–Grade 12* ("WIDA ELD Standards"), Board of Regents of the University of Wisconsin System, on behalf of the WIDA Consortium (2012), www.wida.us.

# The Standards for Mathematical Practice

As mentioned earlier, we find the Standards of Mathematical Practice (SMP) to be invaluable as a framework for understanding students' mathematical thinking and for gauging possible instructional interventions to enrich that thinking further. The SMP also seem particularly suitable for gauging *potential* in student thinking, because development of a particular mathematical practice can be traced from early stages up to more advanced stages, a factor of great importance for mathematics teachers of ELs.

The tasks and student work examples used in this chapter relate in key ways to SMP 1, 2, 6, and 7. (See the following table for a list of the eight SMP.) Student work on other tasks might touch on different standards, depending on the tasks' particular demands on thinking. With that in mind, and on the basis of our experiences working with teachers and students around the SMP, we have listed, for each SMP, several possible features of evidence that might appear in student work, in particular when visual representations are involved. The list is not intended to be comprehensive. Rather, we hope you will add to it through your own experiences, with colleagues, analyzing ELs' student work on mathematics tasks.

| Standards of Mathematical Practice | Possible Evidence in Student Work Related to the SMP |
|---|---|
| **SMP 1** <br> Make sense of problems and persevere in solving them. | • Revises diagrams, which implies perseverance. <br> • Comments and labels appear to show effort to make sense of the relationships among the givens. <br> • Through comments and questions, tries to make sense of someone else's solution. |
| **SMP 2** <br> Reason abstractly and quantitatively. | • Connects parts of visual representations with corresponding parts in the statement of the task, demonstrating the "contextualizing" and "decontextualizing" mentioned in SMP text. <br> • Shows indications of recognizing relationships among quantities in the task or among geometric figures. <br> • States a generalization about mathematical relationships in the task. <br> • Attempts to write about the relationships among quantities or geometric figures. |

| **SMP 3**<br>Construct viable arguments and critique the reasoning of others. | • Attempts to convince, in speaking or writing.<br>• Challenges reasoning in others' solutions. |
|---|---|
| **SMP 4**<br>Model with mathematics. | • Appears to attend to how well her/his representation of the problem captures all the key information about quantities (or geometric properties) and relationships.<br>• Translates a visual representation into a symbolic representation (or vice versa). |
| **SMP 5**<br>Use appropriate tools strategically. | • For quantitative tasks, uses diagramming as a thinking tool, or, in geometry, uses tools such as paper folding. |
| **SMP 6**<br>Attend to precision. | • Attempts to use academic language to describe properties and relationships.<br>• Attempts to bring precision to diagrams, such as showing the relative sizes of and relationships between quantities.<br>• Makes use of precise definitions. |
| **SMP 7**<br>Look for and make use of structure. | • In geometry, thinks about structure of the figures in the task; for example, attempts to decompose an irregular polygon into all right triangles.<br>• In quantitative tasks, apparently tries to exploit the structure of the chosen diagrams—e.g., calculating areas of subsections of an array diagram. |
| **SMP 8**<br>Look for and express regularity in repeated reasoning. | • Appears to generalize a procedure used in solving the task.<br>• Appears to recognize that one kind of diagram may be better to use than another, depending on the type of task. |

# Examples

To illustrate the conditions and features for learning from student-work analysis, consider the following examples of tasks and how we can analyze the visual representations and work produced when working on the tasks.

## How Many People?

Recall the How Many People? problem from Chapter 2. You saw one possible representation in that chapter, but how else might you represent it?

---

### How Many People?
The town of Medtown has three times the population of Carburg.
The *difference* in the number of people in the two towns is 2184 people.
**Create a diagram that helps you know how many people live in each town.**

---

In order to work on a diagram or visual representation for this task, it is necessary to identify the important quantities and relationships in the task and determine how to represent them visually so that they can be "seen." This task explicitly prompts making sense of the quantities and their relationships in a problem situation, which is a practice a mathematically proficient student exhibits when reasoning abstractly and quantitatively (SMP 2). In addition, sometimes the very process of diagramming can help with SMP 1, *Make sense of problems and persevere in solving them.* For example, creating a working diagram can make visible the words in the problem, "The town of Medtown has three times more people than Carburg," as in the diagram on the left.

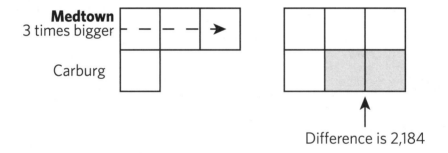

Difference is 2,184

Analyzing the work presented in this diagram reveals the use of area measurement to represent "three times bigger" and also reveals evidence of how the problem solver was engaging in the SMP. First, by attaching the horizontal arrow, it seems the problem solver who produced this work was expressing Mathematical Practice 6, *Attend to precision*, to convey to others which figure represents Medtown's size in comparison with Carburg's size. This problem solver went one step further, representing the difference between the two sizes as shown here. By representing the difference this way, he or she revealed a hidden relationship among the quantities, namely, that the difference, 2184, is actually half the size of the sum of the two populations. Use of color coding in diagramming problems can help with both precision

(SMP 6) and quantitative reasoning (SMP 2). (While precision is often associated with use of language, it should be noted that mathematical precision also comes to the surface when creating diagrams that show the relative sizes of and relationships between quantities, making it possible for others to understand the thinking behind the diagramming. Thus, one should attend to precision in both the doing of the mathematics and communicating mathematically.)

The second diagram (see following) was created by a different person solving the task. Analyzing this work reveals that the color coding (represented by shading here) showed how the thinking occurred in two steps: setting out the relationship between the two populations, and then representing the difference. Altogether, the color coding precisely distinguished the different quantities from each other and helped in revealing relationships among the quantities: It revealed both that the size of Carburg's population is 1/4 of the sum of the sizes of Carburg and Medtown, and it is also 1/2 the difference, 2184. That was enough information to reason from the related quantities to the correct answer to the question, 4368.

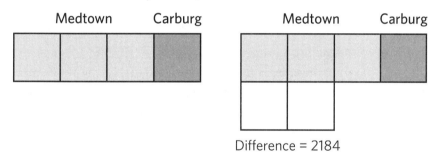

Difference = 2184

## Rita's Reading

Here is a task from our work: *Rita has read 224 pages of her book. She has 1/5 of the book left to read. What is the total number of pages in the book?*

This task was used when we were formally studying EL student mathematical thinking and use of visual representations. So, the type of student work shown next is typical of that generated from a research context, not a regular classroom, but it is still instructive in regard to how we can learn by analyzing student work.

We were interested in seeing how ELs participating in the study would approach this problem, on their own and in pairs. We were limited by the research interview protocol in how much we could influence the students' thinking; thus, it was a different engagement with the solvers than teachers might have in their classrooms.

In their written responses, several students drew representations of the problem like this, and they went no further toward solving the problem:

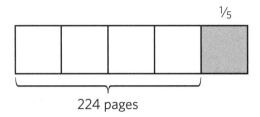

224 pages

At a superficial glance, it could appear that the students made no progress. There is a clear representation of the information in the problem. Unfortunately, there is no answer offered for the problem question nor a possible route toward finding the answer.

We can use the Standards of Mathematical Practice—our framework for "mathematical thinking that is valued"—as a lens to see potential in the partial response, in particular, Mathematical Practice 2, *Reasoning abstractly and quantitatively*. The student's visual representation of the problem portrays a relationship between the quantities "number of pages read" and "number of pages left to read" and appears to imply the relationship: "number of pages read" plus "number of pages left to read" equals "number of pages in the entire book." Finally, the concise and clear representation of the information in the problem suggests Mathematical Practice 6, *Attend to precision*.

One measure of the reasoning potential in a student response to a mathematics task, as well as the potential for growth in mathematical communication, is the degree to which the teacher can imagine questions that might propel the student's reasoning, as well as mathematical communication, to the next level. In the current example, seeing how the visual representation might shine a light on the relationships just mentioned, a teacher might ask: "Where in the diagram is the total number of pages in the entire book?" Or, "Can your diagram help you determine how many pages are in the one-fifth left to read?" A bit more leading, and, therefore, not ideal for fostering independent reasoning, is the question, "If this is ⅕ of the book, what fraction of the book does the quantity 224 pages represent?" For some students it may be just the right nudge to see how to make helpful connections among different quantities in a task statement. With ELs, particularly at lower English language proficiency levels, teachers analyzing this work may consider ways they could employ different language access and language production strategies to prompt responses to these questions. For example, the teacher might decide to write "$1/5$ of the book equals _____ pages," or "$4/5$ of the book equals _____ pages" and ask the ELs to complete the sentence frame. Student responses to these questions and sentence starters could provide teachers further evidence of how mathematical communication is developing among students, particularly English learners.

Ultimately, the purpose of analyzing student work, whether teachers are by themselves or in professional learning settings, should be to inform instruction, and that is how we use student-work analysis in our work with teachers: informing instruction, based on evidence of deficits, competence, and potential in mathematical thinking and communication.

## What Is the Area?

Consider this geometric reasoning task:

---

### What Is the Area?

What is the area of the triangle below? Show your work.

---

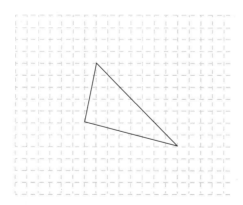

Now take an analytical look at this student's response, based on work produced by students in the classroom of one of our collaborating teachers. The response is by a student considered early intermediate to intermediate in English language proficiency in speaking and writing.

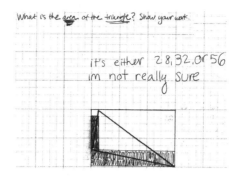

On the surface, even though the student underlined "area" and "triangle," it may appear that the student had little understanding of the concept of area and was doing what many students will do in challenging area tasks: Make the task about numbers, and try to find one that "works."

Using the Standards of Mathematical Practice as a lens when analyzing this student work, however, it is noteworthy that the student seems to see and attend to geometric figures like rectangles surrounding and overlapping the triangle and even seems to try dividing the triangle into figures that are friendlier to measure, like right triangles aligned with the grid. All of this is consistent with SMP 7, *Look for and make use of structure.* Further, there seems to be consistent use of the grid as a measurement tool, which suggests SMP 5, *Use appropriate tools strategically.*

## My Tunes

In Chapter 1, we related how we have dealt with middle-grade students' relative unfamiliarity with visual representations, namely, we have asked students to analyze fictional students' use of visual representations to solve tasks. We have noted a double benefit for ELs in these tasks in which they are asked to analyze others' reasoning: First, they see, analyze to understand, and may emulate examples of how visual representations can be valuable problem-solving tools; second, we have noted that this kind of task seems to free students to practice language more, possibly because the cognitive demands of analysis are less than those of problem solving.

Thus, for the benefit of English learners, we bolster these analytic reasoning tasks with language prompts using devices like sentence starters, so the resulting student work has ample examples of student use of mathematical language. For that reason, when teachers analyze students' "analyses," they have an opportunity to examine ELs' mathematical reasoning, as well as their mathematical communication.

Remember: We do *not* ask students to solve this task; instead, they are expected to put all their attention on how Estella used diagrams to think about it and, using sentence starters, to communicate their answers to our questions.

To ensure that ELs can access the task and to respond to the prompts to write, we used several language strategies to help them identify important information and the purpose of the task. (We will discuss these supports more in the next chapter.)

Below is the task that students worked on, namely, analyzing Estella's solution of the My Tunes problem. Typically, students discussed the questions in pairs, then completed the writing parts individually. Part C of the task is the place students could record words from a Co-constructed Word Bank (see Chapter 4, page 81, for more on this strategy). To provide support for ELs to engage successfully with a task like analyzing Estella's work on the My Tunes problem, we find it important to scaffold with both language access and language production strategies. In this case, we hope to increase access by separating each of Estella's steps and, at each step, prompting production with a sentence starter. Development of a Co-constructed Word Bank can serve both purposes—access and production—by helping students single out words that will be important to understand for describing Estella's thinking and then encouraging students to use those words in their writing.

---

### My Tunes

Dario, Aziza, and Cassie bought songs online from My Tunes.
Dario bought 45 more songs than Aziza.
Aziza bought 15 more songs than Cassie.
Together they bought 300 songs. How many songs did Dario buy?

---

## Analyze the diagrams that Estella created for this problem.

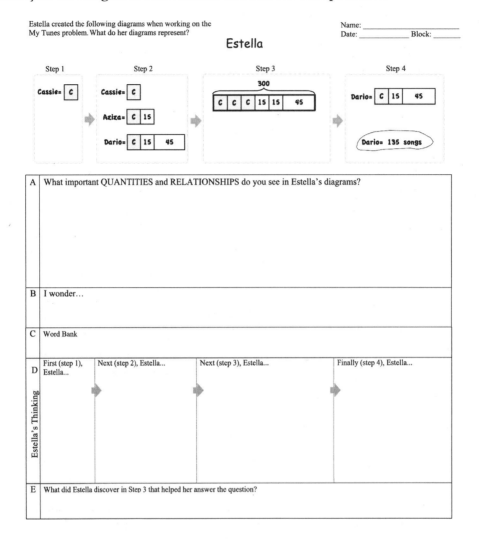

Studying students' communication can reveal both growth in mathematical communication as well as aspects of the mathematics that confuse individual students. To illustrate these benefits, we show three samples of the type of student work we have seen on the Estella task. Each of the samples represents work we have seen from English learners at early intermediate to intermediate English proficiency in speaking and writing. All show they can write in complete, or nearly complete, sentences, and they use mathematical phrases like "how many each has," "has more than," and "total."

## Student Work Example 1

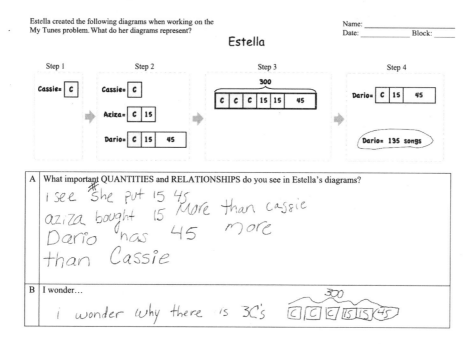

Estella created the following diagrams when working on the My Tunes problem. What do her diagrams represent?

Name: _____
Date: _____ Block: _____

### Estella

| A | What important QUANTITIES and RELATIONSHIPS do you see in Estella's diagrams? |

i see she put 15 45
aziza bought 15 More than cassie
Dario has 45 more
than Cassie

| B | I wonder... |

i wonder why there is 3C's

In Parts A and B of the task, we see this student recording important information from the problem statement, with some possible confusion about the relationship between Cassie's amount and Dario's. Further, the "I wonder" sentence starter prompts a candid and clear reflection by the student: "I wonder why there is 3 Cs," and the student shows by picture exactly which 3 Cs are meant. With this wondering in mind, this student's teacher could lead a potentially productive class discussion, which might embrace both problem solving and algebraic thinking. For example, the teacher might draw attention to how Estella may have been thinking about the C: "Why did Estella write Aziza's amount with a C and a 15?" "What is the relationship between Cassie's number of songs and Aziza's?" "How do Estella's diagrams show this relationship?"

## Student Work Example 2

Estella created the following diagrams when working on the
My Tunes problem. What do her diagrams represent?

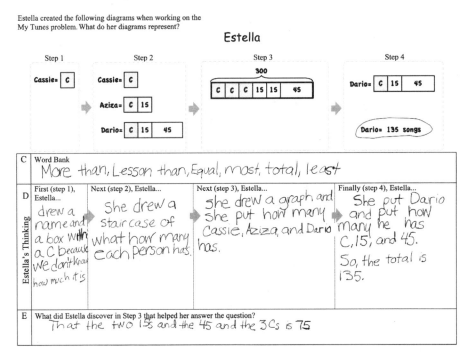

For Part C, this student has listed the words and phrases from the Co-constructed Word Bank (with a slight error: "lesson than" instead of "less than"). The six terms in the word bank reflect the recommendation that the list be compact enough to be useful to students. Teachers often tell students they should use one or more of the terms in the list as they complete the writing prompts. This student does use "total" in the last cell—Step 4. The student also takes a fairly literal approach to describing each of the four steps of Estella's progress, starting with Step 1, "drew a name and a box with a C because we don't know how much it is." This is followed in Step 2 by the student using an evocative metaphor, which does seem to take in Estella's underlying thinking: "She drew a staircase of what how many each person has." In some student work it is evident that students are entirely literal in describing the steps, while in others, like in this example, it seems the students mix the literal with interpretation. In any case, a literal approach is fine, because in reviewing the steps with the entire class, the teacher can add interpretive questions, for example, "Where in Step 3's diagram is Aziza's amount? Dario's amount? Why can Estella combine terms like that?"

This student's response in Part E is confusing to interpret: "that the two 15s and the 45 and the 3 Cs is 75." The teacher likely can help the student by asking him/her to elaborate on how the diagram in Step 3 leads to seeing the number 75. Apparently, this student has done some analysis that does not show up in the wording.

## Student Work Example 3

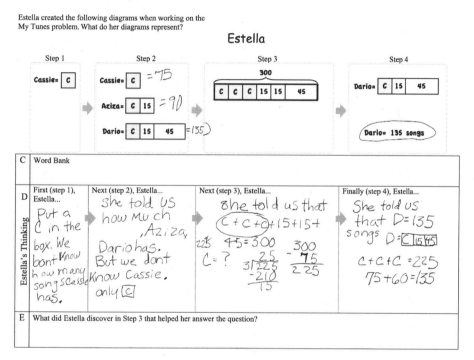

Example 3 starts with the student describing Step 1 as "put a C in the box. We don't know how many songs Cassie has." The description of Step 2 also appears to stick with describing what Estella did. In Step 3, however, the student appears to dive in with her/his interpretation, even translating the juxtaposition of the elements of the Step 3 diagram as implying addition: "She told us that C + C + C + 15 + 15 + 45 = 300." Then the student continues to calculate and even returns to Step 2 and insert amounts for Cassie, Aziza, and Dario in the picture. Unlike Example 2, the student in this third example does not try to use much academic language in the descriptions, but the teacher could amend that by asking the student to describe verbally the thinking behind the interpretation of Step 3, for example, "How do you know Estella was adding all those together?" or "What does the 300 represent in Estella's picture?"

# Analyzing Your Students' Work

We believe that evaluating students' work well places a high value on taking an inquiry stance toward the work. This means, most of all, corralling inclinations to carry foregone conclusions to the process. Rather than letting foregone conclusions hold sway, we urge those analyzing students' work to distinguish between *evidence* and *inference*, that is, distinguishing between what I see/hear (the evidence) and what I infer from that evidence.

We are not saying that making quick inferences is a bad thing. Making quick inferences is part of the human condition, a survival mechanism developed through evolution to allow us to determine threats quickly. It also can be a trap, if relied on too heavily. Our experience can lead us to see what we've seen before—and nothing new. Einstein was supposed to have said that "it is the theory which decides what we can see." That is the trap, and it is particularly problematic in diagnosing problems or making important choices.[4] Analyzing student work involves both diagnosis and making instructional choices, so it can invite falling into this trap. The way to manage the trap is to practice a slower, more inquiry-based way of analyzing. This can lead to new ways of seeing students and their potential.

Becoming thoughtful about separating inferences from evidence takes time and practice. Our emphasis on giving equal weight to evidence and inference in analyzing students' mathematical work is based on the assumption that teachers will have the time to look at student work with an eye toward recognizing potential that can be exploited instructionally—for example, in regularly scheduled professional development or study group sessions with colleagues.[5] We recognize that collaborative analysis of student work may not always be possible for teachers. Time for professional development may be reserved for mandated staff development. However, we do believe that distinguishing between evidence and inferences drawn from evidence is a very important as well as valuable use of time. The issue of jumping

---

[4] The issue has been discussed by authors in other professions, as in the books *Thinking Fast, Thinking Slow* by psychologist Daniel Kahneman, and, in medicine, *How Doctors Think* by Jerome Groopman.

[5] In thinking about setting up collaborative analysis of student work, it may be worth remembering that many districts are avid to have ELL-focused staff development. Often, the design is entrusted to ESL specialists, who may be eager to learn of ways to put this training in the context of content disciplines like mathematics. You can look for opportunities to connect with them.

to conclusions can be particularly hazardous in the case of English learners since, as mentioned in Chapter 1, it is easy for educators to mistakenly see language deficiencies as hurdles precluding ELs from doing challenging mathematics.

## Reflection Tools

The reflection tool we put together to support analyzing student work has two versions: one for geometric reasoning tasks and one for tasks with more of a numerical/quantitative flavor. Furthermore, they can both be used to analyze student work where students are generating their own visual representations to solve problems and where students are analyzing sample visual representations.

### Reflection Tool for Geometric Tasks

| Questions to consider for analysis | Describe your student's understanding of the use of geometric drawings to solve this task. What does your student notice? What are your *inferences* based on that evidence? | |
|---|---|---|
| What is evidence of student understanding *about how to represent geometric properties and relationships?* Examples of types of evidence:<br>• Recognizes significance of an existing feature in a geometric figure, such as a line, shading, or an arrow<br>• Labels drawing<br>• Representations for *all* important properties or relationships | Evidence: | Inference: |
| How did the student *use a geometric drawing* to solve the task? Examples of types of evidence:<br>• Noticed or drew additional geometric features to create or reveal a property or relationship<br>• Described how drawing leads to solution | Evidence: | Inference: |

*Continued*

| Questions to consider for analysis | Describe your student's understanding of the use of geometric drawings to solve this task. What does your student notice? What are your *inferences* based on that evidence? | |
|---|---|---|
| How did the student *use mathematical terms or phrases or sentences* to convey information about the mathematics, the drawing, or his/her reasoning about the task?<br><br>Examples of types of evidence:<br>• Labels or mathematical terms within a geometric drawing<br>• Complete sentences about reasoning | Evidence: | Inference: |
| After reviewing the student's work, what are you still wondering about his/her mathematical thinking, geometric drawing, or language use? | | |

## Reflection Tool for Numerical/Quantitative Tasks

| Questions to consider for analysis | Describe your student's understanding of how to use diagrams to solve the task. What does your student notice? What are your *inferences* based on that evidence? | |
|---|---|---|
| What is evidence of student understanding *about how to represent quantities and relationships*?<br><br>Examples of types of evidence:<br>• Correct representation of individual quantities<br>• Labels for quantities<br>• Representations for *all* important quantities or relationships<br>• Diagrams drawn with appropriate proportions | Evidence: | Inference: |
| How did the student use a diagram to solve the task?<br><br>Examples of types of evidence:<br>• Diagrams versus pictures/ calculations<br>• Description or demonstration of how an answer links to diagram | Evidence: | Inference: |

| Questions to consider for analysis | Describe your student's understanding of how to use diagrams to solve the task. What does your student notice? What are your *inferences* based on that evidence? | |
|---|---|---|
| How did the student *use mathematical terms, phrases, or sentences* to convey information about the mathematics, the diagram, or his/her reasoning about the task?<br><br>Examples of types of evidence:<br>• Labels or mathematical terms within a diagram<br>• Complete sentences about reasoning | Evidence: | Inference: |
| After reviewing the student's work, what are you still wondering about his/her mathematical thinking, diagram of the task, or language use? | | |

## Examples

To demonstrate how you might use these tools for reflection and analysis, we'll share examples using a few different numerical/quantitative tasks. One is the How Many People? task described earlier. Another is Sharing Candies, introduced in Chapter 1. The Ms. Plata's Class and Gas Tank tasks are making their first appearance.

---

### Sharing Candies

**Draw a diagram showing the relationships and quantities.**
**Make your own question for the problem, and answer it using your diagram.**
**Show your work.**

Sara had a bag of candies.

She gave $1/3$ of the candies to Raul.

Then Sara gave $1/4$ of the candies she had left to Jasmine.

After giving candies to Raul and Jasmine, Sara had 24 candies left in her bag.

---

### Ms. Plata's Class

Mr. Copper's and Ms. Plata's math classes both have the same number of students. The ratio of girls to boys in Mr. Copper's class is 3:2. The ratio of girls to boys in Ms. Plata's class is 2:1. Mr. Copper's class has 18 girls.

**How many girls are in Ms. Plata's class?**

### Gas Tank

José's father stops at a gas station to buy gas.

His car has a 16-gallon gas tank. The tank is $3/8$ full.

José's father buys 6 gallons of gas and puts it in the tank.

*After* he buys the gas, what *fraction* of the tank has gas in it?

**Create a diagram that helps you to solve the problem. Show your work.**

The following examples present *possible* evidence from student work on these four tasks and possible inferences about those pieces of evidence that someone might note when analyzing student work on these four tasks. We chose to present a variety of evidence and inference examples drawing on the work of different students on different tasks. Each bullet showing an example of evidence in any of the charts comes from a different student—they are not all from the same student.

### Sharing Candies

| Questions to consider for analysis | Describe *evidence* that you see in student work samples and *inferences* based on that evidence | |
|---|---|---|
| What is evidence of student understanding *about how to represent quantities and relationships*? Examples of types of evidence: <br> • Correct representation of individual quantities <br> • Labels for quantities <br> • Representations for *all* important quantities or relationships <br> • Diagrams drawn with appropriate proportions | Evidence: <br> Student shows $1/2$ and $1/3$ as quantities (as a $1/2$ of 1 or $1/3$ of 1) but not as parts of the whole bag of candy. | Inferences: <br> Student understands the quantity of $1/2$ of 1, but there is not evidence of understanding $1/2$ of a quantity other than 1. |

| How did the student *use a diagram* to solve the Sharing Candies task?<br><br>Examples of types of evidence:<br>• Diagrams versus pictures/calculations<br>• Description or demonstration of how an answer links to a diagram | Evidence:<br>• The diagram shows Jasmine has $1/2$ the amount of candy given to Raul.<br><br>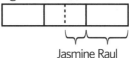<br><br>• The diagram shows all three students' candies and uses color. | Inferences:<br>• Accuracy in the diagram helped the student show relationships to others.<br><br>• Student was trying to represent relationships among quantities. The color may have helped the student see relationships. |
| How did the student *use mathematical terms or phrases or sentences* to convey information about the mathematics, the diagram, or his/her reasoning about the task?<br><br>Examples of types of evidence:<br>• Labels or mathematical terms within a diagram<br>• Complete sentences about reasoning | Evidence:<br>• Student circled the phrase "had left."<br><br>• Student used the phrase "left over": "Sara had 24 left over." | Inferences:<br>• Student identified a phrase that seemed important (not sure if student understands the phrase).<br>• Student understands the phrase *left over* and used it to accurately identify the amount that Sara had. |

## Ms. Plata's Class

| Questions to consider for analysis | Describe *evidence* that you see in student work samples and *inferences* based on that evidence | |
|---|---|---|
| What is evidence of student understanding *about how to represent quantities and relationships*?<br>Examples of types of evidence:<br>• Correct representation of individual quantities<br>• Labels for quantities<br>• Representations for *all* important quantities or relationships<br>• Diagrams drawn with appropriate proportions | Evidence:<br>• The student created a tape diagram for each class:<br><br>    Ms. Plata's Class<br><br>    Mr. Cooper's Class<br><br>• Student labeled parts of the diagram to show boys and girls in each class. | Inference:<br>• Student made the tapes the same size, showing he or she understood that both classes had same number of students.<br><br>• Other students appeared to understand student's diagram. Clear labeling really helped. |
| How did the student *use a diagram* to solve the Ms. Plata's Class task?<br>Examples of types of evidence:<br>• Diagrams versus pictures/calculations<br>• Description or demonstration of how an answer links to diagram | Evidence:<br>• Student's diagram of Mr. Copper's class (where the ratio of girls to boys is 3:2) shows five equal parts.<br><br>    \| G \| G \| G \| B \| B \| | Inference:<br>• Student reasoned that the ratio of 3:2 needed five parts. Diagram suggests a solution path. |
| How did the student *use mathematical terms or phrases or sentences* to convey information about the mathematics, the diagram, or his/her reasoning about the task?<br>Examples of types of evidence:<br>• Labels or mathematical terms within a diagram<br>• Complete sentences about reasoning | Evidence:<br>• Student rewrote the "ratio of girls to boys is 3:2" as "3 girls/2 boys" and the "ratio of girls to boys is 2:1" as "2 girls/1 boy." | Inference:<br>• Student understands the ratio 3:2 as relating the number of girls and boys. |

## Gas Tank

| Questions to consider for analysis | Describe *evidence* that you see in student work samples and *inferences* based on that evidence | |
|---|---|---|
| What is evidence of student understanding *about how to represent quantities and relationships*?<br>Examples of types of evidence:<br>• Correct representation of individual quantities<br>• Labels for quantities<br>• Representations for *all* important quantities or relationships<br>• Diagrams drawn with appropriate proportions | Evidence:<br>• Student drew a rectangle and shaded in $3/8$ of it.<br>• Student revised diagram to make each eighth (or sixteenth) about the same size, and the tank "looks" like it is about $3/8$ full.<br> | Inference:<br>• Student understood that $3/8$ of the tank was full to begin with.<br>• This attempt to make parts of the diagram precise in proportions likely helped others make sense of the solution. |
| How did the student *use a diagram* to solve the Gas Tank task?<br>Examples of types of evidence:<br>• Diagrams versus pictures/calculations<br>• Description or demonstration of how an answer links to the diagram | Evidence:<br>• Student divided the rectangle into 16 cells and shaded six in one color and six in another color.<br> | Inference:<br>• Student represented relationships among quantities. The color may have helped the student see relationships. |
| How did the student *use mathematical terms, phrases, or sentences* to convey information about the mathematics, the diagram, or his/her reasoning about the task?<br>Examples of types of evidence:<br>• Labels or mathematical terms within a diagram<br>• Complete sentences about reasoning | Evidence:<br>• Student circled the phrase "fraction of."<br><br><br>• Student wrote: "$3/4$ of the tank had gas in it." | Inferences:<br>• Student identified a phrase that seemed important (not sure if student understands the phrase).<br>• Student understands the phrase "of the tank" to mean a part of the tank and used it to accurately identify the fraction of tank that was full. |

## How Many People?

| Questions to consider for analysis: | Describe *evidence* that you see in student work samples and *inferences* based on that evidence | |
|---|---|---|
| What is evidence of student understanding *about how to represent quantities and relationships*? Examples of types of evidence:<br>• Correct representation of individual quantities<br>• Labels for quantities<br>• Representations for *all* important quantities or relationships<br>• Diagrams drawn with appropriate proportions | Evidence:<br>• Diagram to show number of people in Medtown is three times as long as diagram to show number of people Carburg.<br><br>Medtown<br><br>Carburg | Inference:<br>• I'm guessing this visual representation of "three times" conveys the relationship to my students better than something like $M = 3C$. |
| How did the student *use a diagram* to solve the How Many People? task? Examples of types of evidence:<br>• Diagrams versus pictures/calculations<br>• Description or demonstration of how an answer links to diagram | Evidence:<br><br>Medtown<br><br>Carburg    2184 | Inference:<br>• Diagram suggests a solution path by noting that the difference between the towns is equal to two-thirds of Medtown (or twice the size of Carburg). |
| How did the student *use mathematical terms, phrases, or sentences* to convey information about the mathematics, the diagram, or his/her reasoning about the task? Examples of types of evidence:<br>• Labels or mathematical terms within a diagram<br>• Complete sentences about reasoning | Evidence:<br>• Student circled the word "difference" and wrote "subtract."<br>• Student used the word "combined": "Medtown and Carburg combined are 4368." | Inference:<br>• Student relates difference to subtraction.<br>• Student used the word "combined" accurately to describe the total number of people. |

In our experience, it sometimes happens that two teachers in a group will have very different, even opposing, inferences from the same evidence in a student's work. This is almost always valuable in learning, because each person must talk through the steps he or she took to go from evidence to inference. It is especially important for teachers of English learners to be open to the possibility of different inferences, because language deficiencies often can fog up interpretations of students' mathematical thinking.

## Noticing Potential

As we hope this chapter demonstrated, ELs' diagram-enriched work on challenging mathematics tasks can point teachers toward recognizing potential and discovering ways to widen access. Furthermore, when groups of teachers from the same district—or even better, the same school—analyze this work together, fair chances for EL students to succeed will multiply.

We have learned that several conditions seem conducive for teachers to become adept at noticing competence and potential in student work:

- Mathematics tasks that elicit student reasoning

- Time to analyze student work outside of classroom instruction

- Opportunities to analyze and discuss the student work with colleagues, for example, mathematics coaches, ESL specialists, or fellow teachers

Chapters 1 and 5 have much to say about the first point, so we will not elaborate here but only reiterate that we place a high value on capturing evidence of student *reasoning*, and so we believe the tasks behind the student work should be able to elicit mathematical reasoning from all students.

Regarding the second point, time analyzing student work outside of instruction allows the teacher to be free from distractions caused by the immediate needs and demands emanating from a roomful of students. This time away from instruction can be combined with lesson planning. For example, you can profitably analyze several samples of EL student work from the previous lesson and reflect on how the evidence impacts your planning for the next lesson.

The third point emphasizes the value of variety in perspective. We have been lucky to work with groups that included mathematics teachers, ESL specialists, mathematics coaches, and building administrators. In such groups, the different perspectives bring different lenses to considering EL student work, so questions like "I wonder why he didn't go further with that line of thinking" or "Why would she have written that?" can elicit insightful answers, suggestions, and further questions to investigate. ESL specialists might say things like: "That task statement has a sentence with a clause within a clause. Students at the beginner level of English proficiency will really struggle with that." That sort of information can inspire mathematics teachers to pay greater heed to potential complications in written tasks. In return, mathematics teachers can show ESL specialists how use of diagrams and other mathematical drawings can retain the mathematical challenge of a task, while lightening the verbal demand.

Listening to those exchanges has been one of the ways we have been motivated to integrate language strategies, along with visual representations, into mathematics lessons. We believe that ELs can learn mathematical communication while engaged in mathematical thinking. The next chapter, Chapter 4, describes what we have learned.

# Chapter 4

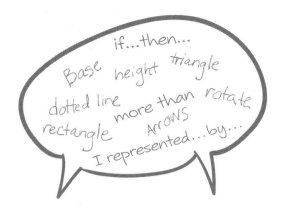

# Developing Language in Context

Students face considerable but not insurmountable challenges when learning and doing mathematics in a classroom environment where the primary language is one in which they are not yet fluent. As described earlier in this book, in our work with mathematics teachers of ELs we emphasize the regular use of challenging mathematical tasks embedded in instructional routines that integrate both multimodal representation—especially mathematical visual representations as described in Chapter 2—and supports for the development of academic language. The instructional routines that embody these principles allow teachers and their students to focus on the key elements of their mathematical work and communication and are described in more detail in Chapter 6. In this chapter, we will explore more deeply some of the specific supports for the development of academic language that we have found to be fruitful in our work with teachers.

## Developing Academic Language

First, it is important to note what we *do not* mean when we talk about "developing academic language."

We do not mean to suggest that all that students need is to learn a particular mathematical vocabulary. Speaking mathematically (or writing mathematically) and understanding what you hear or read of others' mathematical talk involves many components. The words and phrases in mathematics take on a variety of forms: "words referring to thinking and communicating (e.g., *analysis, deny*); words common across subjects but with different meanings depending on subject (e.g., *base, element*); and words that have common meanings that differ from discipline-specific meanings (e.g., *prove, property*)" (Driscoll, Heck, and Malzahn 2012, 170).[1] Furthermore, in order to take part in mathematical discourse practices in the classroom and fully develop mathematical ideas, students must be able to share their own mathematical thinking in ways that are understandable to others and to understand the mathematical communication that others share. This involves more than knowing certain vocabulary words. Sometimes this necessitates communicating in more informal language or, alternatively, in a student's first language (if permitted and if others understand that language or are informed of what information was exchanged). More precise mathematical terminology can then be connected to the ideas that students have expressed. Sometimes pictures, gestures, or diagrams can express mathematical ideas that are difficult to convey using words alone and also act as a reference point for verbal expression of an idea. This mathematical communication entails far more than mathematical vocabulary; it covers norms for mathematical communication (e.g., how to build a mathematical argument), sentence structures (e.g., if . . . then . . .), skills to express developing mathematical ideas, and skills to support and question mathematical ideas expressed by others.

We also do not mean that support for academic language should take the form of separating language work from mathematical work. Unfortunately, instead of integrating language supports into mathematics, some schools address ELs' needs by separating language work from mathematics work (Firestone, Martinez, and Polovsky 2006).[2] ELs' regular participation in

---

[1]  M. Driscoll, D. Heck, and K. Malzahn, "Knowledge for Teaching English Language Learners Mathematics," in *Beyond Good Teaching: Advancing Mathematics Education for ELLs*, eds. S. Celedón-Pattichis and N. Ramirez (Reston, VA: National Council of Teachers of Mathematics, 2012).

[2]  W. A. Firestone, M. C. Martinez, and T. Polovsky, *Teaching Mathematics and Science to English Language Learners: The Experience of Four New Jersey Elementary Schools*. New Jersey Math Science Partnership (2006). Retrieved from http://hub.mspnet.org/index.cfm/13070.

"explaining solution processes, describing conjectures, proving conclusions and presenting arguments" both orally and in writing is imperative (Moschkovich 1999, 11).[3] In this chapter, we present how to integrate language with mathematical work in ways that benefit all students. Our goal is always to support students to access the mathematical work of the classroom and to be *active producers of the mathematical work and communication.* Mathematics is not a passive subject: Doing mathematical work requires being part of the mathematical discourse practices in the classroom and students of *all English language proficiency levels* must be actively engaged in doing mathematical work. Communication plays a big role in some of the key mathematical habits to be fostered in students, for example, constructing mathematical arguments, critiquing the reasoning of others, and being precise in mathematical communication. (These mathematical habits are captured well in the CCSS Standards for Mathematical Practice, specifically SMP 3, *Construct viable arguments and critique the reasoning of others*, and SMP 6, *Look for and make use of precision.*)

## The Role of Language Support Strategies

Language support strategies can reduce some linguistic demands inherent in communicating about mathematics and promote students' language production. In our own work, we have found that ELs benefitted from sustained supports for communicating about their reasoning and developing academic vocabulary *in the context of mathematical work.* The following research-based instructional strategies are designed to promote students' *access to* or *understanding* of language involved in a mathematical task or lesson, or students' *production* of mathematical communication as they work on that task or lesson, or both. These strategies can each be integrated into lessons to support ELs' understanding and participation and can be tailored to the particular needs of individual students or the class as a whole, for example, with consideration for the English language proficiency levels of students or for the mix of first languages that are present in a given class. These strategies, organized by their primary purpose, are shown in the following table.

---

[3] J. Moschkovich, "Supporting the Participation of English Language Learners in Mathematical Discussions," *For the Learning of Mathematics* 19, no. 1 (1999): 11–19.

| Primarily Supporting Access to Task Language | Supporting Both Access to Task Language and Production of Language | Primarily Providing Support for Producing Language |
|---|---|---|
| Three Reads | Differentiated Teacher Questions | Sentence Starters and Frames |
| Acting Out and Realia | Frayer Model | Co-constructed Word Bank |
| Clarifying Vocabulary | Teacher Revoicing | Pairs Work |

Note that all the strategies in some sense support access to the mathematical work in the classroom and, therefore, production of mathematical work by the students. Their classification as supporting access to language and/or production of language has to do with the purpose that is generally at the forefront when using the strategy.

## Additional Concerns

Two other factors affect language access and production but are not directly addressed in this chapter's collection of instructional strategies. The first pertains to the language used in mathematics tasks and key features of task language that teachers should attend to (e.g., verb tense and phrasing). Chapter 5 discusses this factor in some depth. The second factor relates to how teachers go about helping ELs communicate mathematically on a regular basis—both talking and writing—in ways that support those students to improve and revise their communication through drafting and revising. Mathematics teachers can act as guides as they help ELs alter both spoken and written language. Supporting ELs' development of spoken and written language can lead students to communicate their mathematical thinking with more detail, participate more readily in mathematical discussions, and increase their opportunities for further mathematical learning through participation and reflection.[4] Therefore, when working with ELs, it is important to encourage continued communication, even as a student is developing and has not yet mastered vocabulary or sentence structure. This means that you would allow a student to mispronounce a word as she drafts her spoken ideas, for example saying, "parallela," or misspell as he drafts his response; then, either in spoken or written word, the student can revise his or her work.[5] This idea of drafting and revising talk and writing is not detailed as a

---

[4] L. L. Khisty and K. Chval, "Pedagogic Discourse and Equity in Mathematics: When Teachers' Talk Matters," *Mathematics Education Research Journal* 14, no. 3 (2002): 154–68.

[5] J. N. Moschkovich, "Supporting the Participation of English Language Learners in Mathematical Discussions," *For the Learning of Mathematics* 19, no. 1 (1999): 11–19.

specific strategy, but we suggest that you consider how to give ELs these opportunities within the different strategies we describe.

## Strategies for Language Support

To meet ELs' needs it is necessary to "expand what we know about good teaching" and develop mathematics teaching practices that "specifically address the language demands of students who are developing skill in listening, speaking, reading, and writing in a second language while learning mathematics" (Celedón-Pattichis and Ramirez 2012, 1).[6] The strategies outlined in this chapter are some of the supports we have found helpful for teachers to integrate into students' mathematical work to address these demands. Integrating oral and written English instruction into mathematics and specifically providing structured and scaffolded opportunities to do so align with the recommendations in the IES practice guide, *Teaching Academic Content and Literacy to English Learners in Elementary and Middle School* (Baker et al. 2014).[7]

The following language support strategies are designed to integrate language access and production into mathematical learning. In using language support strategies, it is critical both to think about and attend to your ELs and their unique strengths and challenges and to think about strategies for *classroom* use[8] that can help you facilitate students' communication and continued development. These research- and practice-based strategies highlight mathematical communication and participation and align with current recommendations for supporting language in classroom use.[7] The following sections share the language support strategies and ideas for their classroom implementation. Following those sections are additional details for how to choose a strategy to use.

---

[6]  S. Celedón-Pattichis and N. G. Ramirez, Eds., *Beyond Good Teaching: Advancing Mathematics Education for ELLs* (Reston, VA: National Council of Teachers of Mathematics, 2012).

[7]  S. Baker, N. Lesaux, M. Jayanthi, J. Dimino, C. P. Proctor, J. Morris, R. Gersten, K. Haymond, M. J. Kieffer, S. Linan-Thompson, and R. Newman-Gonchar, *Teaching Academic Content and Literacy to English Learners in Elementary and Middle School* (NCEE 2014-4012) (Washington, DC: National Center for Education Evaluation and Regional Assistance (NCEE), Institute of Education Sciences, U.S. Department of Education, 2014). Retrieved from the NCEE website: http://ies.ed.gov/ncee /wwc/publications_reviews.aspx.

[8]  See also K. B. Chval and O. Chávez, "Designing Math Lessons for English Language Learners," *Mathematics Teaching in the Middle School* 17, no. 5 (2011): 261–65.

## Strategies That Primarily Support Access to Language

### Three Reads

The Three Reads strategy is a language access support that can help ELs make sense of mathematics text such as word problems. It is designed for use during the sense making or launch of a mathematics task. It is based on the idea that reading a math word problem requires a different approach than reading other prose, in part because the purpose (e.g., the question to be answered) typically does not appear until the end of the passage. Because the reader does not know the purpose until the end, it can be difficult to determine the importance of the information within the text. In addition, math problem text is often dense and may include unfamiliar academic language. Reading it more than once may strengthen students' understanding.

**Implementation:** The Three Reads strategy uses three readings of the text in order to make sense of the material:

1.  The first read is to get a sense of context in order to understand the "story" or big idea of the text. Students should not focus on the quantities or relationships between them during this reading.

2.  The second read is to discern the question or purpose of the text. The problem is read again in its entirety, looking specifically for information about what needs to be answered or done to be successful.

3.  The third read of the text is to gather important information that is needed to solve the problem or achieve the purpose of the task, such as specific quantities and their relationships.

A graphic organizer or template such as the following can be helpful for students using this strategy.

| 1st Read | CONTEXT<br>The problem is about_____. |
|---|---|
| 2nd Read | PURPOSE<br>I need to find out_____. |
| 3rd Read | INFORMATION<br>• <br>• <br>• |

Teachers typically use the Three Reads strategy when introducing a mathematics problem to the class. You can vary your use of this strategy, depending on students' language fluency, and decide whether each of the reads is done out loud or silently, in the full group or in pairs. With a class of strong readers or to differentiate the use of the Three Reads strategy by allowing some students to move at their own pace, students can use the strategy independently. Although the strategy can be successfully used individually or quietly, repeated reading out loud in a group or class context provides additional support to students who are ELs by providing opportunities to hear and see the language multiple times. It is helpful to have several students share their responses for the Three Reads in the full group and to record responses in a place where all students can see them. Having several students share their responses, even if there is some repetition, allows more students to practice their language and allows students to hear the information multiple times and in multiple forms. Consider how and whether to record the different responses and how to indicate, for example, which pieces of "information" shared for the third read are correct or important to keep in mind before moving on to working on the task.

Here is one example that is typical of students' completed Three Reads templates for the Sharing Candies task. Note that in this example, the task did not include a question to answer; instead, students were asked to create and answer their own question (so, the task had a different "purpose" for students).

**Draw a diagram showing the relationships and quantities.**
**Make your own question for the problem and answer it using your diagram.**
**Show your work.**

Sara had a bag of candies.

She gave $\frac{1}{3}$ of the candies to Raul.

Then Sara gave $\frac{1}{4}$ of the candies she had left to Jasmine.

After giving candies to Raul and Jasmine, Sara had 24 candies left in her bag.

| 1ˢᵗ Read | **CONTEXT** |
|---|---|
| | The problem is about ___Sarah and her candy.___ |
| 2ⁿᵈ Read | **PURPOSE** |
| | I need to ___Create a question.___ |
| 3ʳᵈ Read | **INFORMATION** |
| | • Gave 1/3 to Raul. <br> • gave 1/4 to Jasmine. <br> • 24 candies left in bag. |

Looking at what this student wrote in the important information section of the Three Reads chart can help the teacher assess his or her understanding of the task and provide appropriate support. For example, in this student's Three Reads work, the student wrote "gave $1/3$ to Raul" and "gave $1/4$ to Jasmine" but it is unclear whether the student understands what the whole is in each of these cases and that the two wholes are different (based on what amount was left in the bag each time candy was shared).

Another benefit of using this method is that you can use the responses that students recorded on the Three Reads chart to help students analyze the diagrams that they and their peers generate for the task during later full-group sharing and discussion. For example, for the Sharing Candies task, you can call students' attention to a presented diagram for the task and ask "Where in this diagram do you see the 24 candies Sara has left?" while pointing at "Sara had 24 candies left" in the important information section of the Three Reads template.

## Acting Out and Realia

Acting Out and Realia are two related language access supports. Acting Out supports ELs in interpreting text because they are able to watch an enactment of the task context while hearing the language in the task. This active visual demonstration allows ELs to both hear and see the language used. Realia are real objects such as candies, cups, and bags, and they can be used during acting out to help students interpret the context and learn vocabulary by seeing and experiencing "hands-on" objects represented by words in the text.

**Implementation:** Acting Out and Realia as strategies can be used separately. For example, in the launch of the Sharing Candies task, which is about a student sharing different fractions of her candy with other students, a teacher could show students a bag of candy as the task is read, without any acting out, or the teacher and volunteer students could act out the sharing process. Similarly, during a task that includes the word *gallon*, you could bring in a gallon container. You could also implement acting out without realia, for example, in the Sharing Candies task by pretending to share [imaginary] candy without using any candy, small objects, or other realia, or you could ask students to act out the task through pretending to share. While in some cases using realia alone or acting out alone may be most appropriate; when possible, consider combining both strategies since this may provide a more comprehensive language access experience for students who are ELs. When deciding whether or not to implement Acting Out and/or Realia, consider time (i.e., can it conveniently be done in a short amount of time so as not to shortchange time for the mathematical work of the task?) and payoff (i.e., will acting out and/or realia allow students access to the mathematical work that they should be doing that they would not otherwise have had?).

For the Sharing Candies task, both Acting Out and Realia strategies provide specific benefits. The task works well for these strategies in part because it has distinct steps:

1. Sara had a bag of candies.
2. She gave $1/3$ of the candies to Raul.
3. Then she gave $1/4$ of the candies she had left to Jasmine.
4. After giving candies to Raul and Jasmine, Sara had 24 candies left in her bag.

Three students could volunteer to act out these steps. The student acting as Sara would hold a bag of candies and then give some to the student acting as Raul. Then, the "Sara" student would give some to the student acting as Jasmine. The distinct steps allow a narrator to help the flow of action and allow the other students to watch the task being performed. Acting out the steps also helps students to understand this complex algebraic problem, where one-fourth of the two-thirds left were given to Jasmine. In context of the performance, this is much clearer than as written. In addition, in context, the word *left* is about a fraction of an amount and not a direction, such as on the left side of the table. The candy used as realia also helps with performing the story. In the first step of the task, the amount of candy is unknown, and this can be confusing to students when reading the task without realia or acting, but when the sharing is acted out, the unknown bag of candy is placed into context.

The following questions can guide your use of the Acting Out and Realia strategies:

- What context information is most important to convey with acting out and through the use of realia? What contextual information and language must students know to engage in the mathematics of the task?

- Who will perform the acting out? Will the teacher be the lead actor, a director, or a supporting role? Which students (possibly including ELs) will perform, and how will you communicate with them beforehand so they know what to do?

- What realia will be used, and how, to support the context and important language in the task?

- What other supports can be integrated with the experience that provide additional language development support, such as strategies (e.g., Three Reads, Clarifying Vocabulary, Sentence Starters) or props (e.g., name tags, cards with academic language, costumes or accessories, photographs, videos)?

- Which students will benefit from the acting out and/or realia—should this strategy be used in the full class or with small groups or individuals? Should it be used right away, or only if students are confused about the task—and how will I gauge if they are confused by the task?

## Clarifying Vocabulary

Some vocabulary, terms, or phrases in a mathematical task, in particular the meaning of the term or phrase or its use in *mathematics*, may be unfamiliar to students. The Clarifying Vocabulary strategy involves purposeful work by the teacher to help ELs make sense of that language by emphasizing the mathematical terms and phrases and multiple meanings of words in mathematics.[9]

The goal of this strategy is to think carefully about which terms or phrases need clarification and which do not, and when and how during the lesson these terms or phrases should be clarified. When vocabulary and phrases are clarified, it should be to support students' understanding of the mathematics, the task, and the related vocabulary, with a focus on providing students just enough access to the language of the task so they can work toward the mathematics and language objectives of the lesson. Defining terms should not replace students' involvement in the mathematical work of the lesson but instead should help students understand formal or informal definitions of words to strengthen both students'

---

[9] M. Driscoll, D. Heck, and K. Malzahn, "Knowledge for Teaching English Language Learners Mathematics," in *Beyond Good Teaching: Advancing Mathematics Education for ELLs*, eds. S. Celedón-Pattichis and N. Ramirez (Reston, VA: National Council of Teachers of Mathematics, 2012).

communication and their understanding of the task.[10] This strategy ties in with other language strategies described in this chapter, such as the Co-constructed Word Bank, Three Reads, Realia/Acting Out, and the Frayer Model. For example, during enactment of the Three Reads or the Co-constructed Word Bank strategy, opportunities for clarifying language may arise (e.g., the teacher can work with students to clarify important terms when they come up during student sharing). Also, Realia/Acting Out and the Frayer Model are both particular strategies for clarifying language. For example, in the Sharing Candies task, a teacher should decide when to clarify the term *left*. This term could be clarified before, after, or during the reading of the task. Clarifying the term *left* during or after using the Acting Out strategy would allow students to stay involved in the mathematics and in the task, and through learning the term in context, students might have additional ways to clarify the meaning themselves when prompted.

Clarifying key terms may come at a different point in the lesson, and your choice as to when to clarify terms depends on the accessibility of the term and language, students' prior in-class learning, and the mathematical task. For example, consider the How Many People? task:

---

### How Many People?

The population of the town of Medtown is three times the size of the population of the town of Carburg.

The *difference* in the number of people in the two towns is 2,184 people.

How many people live in Medtown and Carburg **combined**?

Create a diagram that helps you to solve the problem. Show your work.

---

New terms in this task could include *population*, *three times the size*, *difference*, *combined*, or *diagram*, and the teacher should think carefully about all of these terms to make decisions about timing and to plan how the term would be clarified to students. Clarifying all terms at the introduction to the task or during the Three Reads strategy may limit students' engagement in the mathematics of the task and place too much of an emphasis on vocabulary. Instead, depending on language abilities and prior in-class instruction,

---

[10] K. B. Chval and O. Chávez, "Designing Math Lessons for English Language Learners," *Mathematics Teaching in the Middle School* 17, no. 5 (2011): 261–65.

you may choose to clarify some terms before the lesson and wait to do other terms as they arise. It may be best to clarify the term *population* in order to give students access to the context of the task and the language so they can work on the mathematics but allow any clarification of the terms *difference* and *combine* to arise during the reading of the task, or even after students have begun solving. Students may be able to infer some or all of the meanings of *difference* and *combined* or may be able to reason as a group about these terms. The teacher could take the opportunity to build and add onto students' reasoning after they have shared. This option for using this strategy would allow the students' own reasoning to remain prominent, and then their reasoning could be related to the specific context. In addition, the term *diagram* may be a term that you want students to define themselves in order to have a working definition that they continue to add to as they work on tasks in class.

In preparing to use and implement this strategy, the emphasis should be on selecting terms and phrases that need clarification, determining what is important for students to know about them, and then incorporating formal and informal definitions, acting out and pictures or realia, gesturing, explicit categorization of action words, and strategic use of color to support clarifying vocabulary.

**Implementation:** The Clarifying Vocabulary strategy should generally be implemented during the sense making or launch of a mathematics task in order to provide all students access to the language in a math task. It may be introduced during the initial phase of a lesson (e.g., during the Three Reads strategy) or whenever teachers feel it fits for their students and the task (e.g., during partner work or in conjunction with creating a Co-constructed Word Bank). Teachers should be alert to highlight and clarify phrases used to describe quantities that will be important to understand, such as *number of* or *amount of*. Other important terms to include are any that have to do with mathematical relationships, such as *more than*. Or, in a geometry context, these words may include *triangle*, *area*, and *square unit*, as well as words students may use to transform the figure such as *rotate*, *reflect*, or *slide*. Additionally, terms such as *left* could be referring to the remaining amount, such as *the amount left in the tank*, or a direction, such as *the triangle on the left*. In reviewing a task, it is important to recognize the terms that may have multiple meanings or a mathematical meaning and discuss the meaning as it relates to the task.

In clarifying terms with students, encourage students to share their understandings of the terms and work to build on their understandings so it includes mathematical meanings that are specific to the task. In addition to having students share their ideas verbally or in writing, we offer a few other techniques to try out when clarifying language including:

- *Gesturing* when illustrating words can support student understanding,[11] particularly of action words. Gesturing emphasizes manipulation and transformation and can be used when describing or analyzing visuals in a geometry context to support student understanding of steps or changes in a visual. When gesturing and clarifying terms with students in general, encourage students to share their understandings of the terms and work to build on their understandings so it includes mathematical meanings that are specific to the task. For example, follow a gesture about "rotating" with a connection to the mathematics of the task as well as a definition, if appropriate. Students can also gesture to illustrate their understanding. Students could use a gesture of bringing their hands together to show "combine" as in the How Many People? task, and a teacher can use one student's gesture with the rest of the class in order to increase all student understanding.

- Categorizing **action words** for operating on geometric visuals (shading, dissecting, rotating, etc.) and discussing these in comparison to nouns (e.g., triangle) may support student understanding and can be supported through gesturing. Distinguishing between action words and nouns may help students in determining next steps in their diagramming or solving. For example, when the task asks a student to dissect a triangle, and when *dissect* and *triangle* are both new terms, thinking about action words and nouns can support students in thinking of what is *being done* (e.g., dissecting) and what it is *being done to* (e.g., the triangle), which in turn can help them make sense of the situation.

- *Color* can help delineate figures or steps in a diagram and clarify what a student is noticing or referring to with words or labels. Teachers can use color deliberately in their own diagramming and encourage students to use color in their diagrams, both in their independent and

---

[11] K. B. Chval and O. Chávez, "Designing Math Lessons for English Language Learners," *Mathematics Teaching in the Middle School* 17, no. 5 (2011): 261–65.

partner work and when sharing their diagrams in full-group discussions. For example, in the Sharing Candies task, color (or shading) can show the tem *left* and relate the fractions to the full bag of candies. In the diagram below, by shading ¹/₃ (the far-left sections of the diagram) and then shading Jasmine's candies and labeling that section, the teacher can show and the student can see what the term *left* represents and means in the mathematical context of the task.

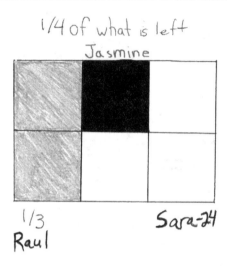

## Strategies That Primarily Support Language Production

### Sentence Starters and Frames

Sentence Starters and Frames are common language production supports that can help ELs communicate mathematically by supporting them as they craft and share their mathematical ideas orally and in writing.[12] Sentence starters are incomplete sentences that students are asked to complete and provide structures for students' writing and speaking. The beginning of the sentence is provided, and the student must add the ending. Sentence frames are a close cousin—they have at least one "blank" to be completed within the middle of the sentence and may include multiple blanks, where sentence starters include only a single blank at the end of the sentence. Sentence frames, therefore, often have an additional layer of complexity but can

---

[12] J. Carr, C. Carroll, S. Cremer, M. Gale, R. Lagunoff, and U. Sexton, *Making Mathematics Accessible to English Learners: A Guidebook for Teachers* (San Francisco, CA: WestEd, 2009).

support students in understanding a particular sentence structure (e.g., if . . . then . . .).

When given a sentence starter or frame, a student does not need to first interpret a question but can instead focus on formulating his or her ideas (e.g., "The amount of [Raul/Jasmine/Sara]'s candies is represented by . . ."). Sentence Starters and Frames can encourage students to practice reading, speaking, and/or writing academic language they may not otherwise use or support them using a specific academic term (e.g., "The *ratio* of girls to boys in Mr. Copper's class is shown by . . . ," "The *ratio* of . . . is shown in the *diagram* by . . .").[13] Providing sentence starters or frames can support students of different language proficiency levels participating in verbal and written mathematical communication. Sentence frames particularly provide support and scaffolding so students can formulate their own ideas using mathematical language within the structure of a sentence, such as "The next time I make a diagram I will . . . because . . ." Both methods support all students participating in verbal and written mathematical communication.

**Implementation:** Sentence Starters and Frames can be used to support students in their individual reflections, partner sharing, and full-group discussions. Sentence starters and frames can have multiple purposes, and when planning, teachers should clarify the purpose for their use of sentence starters.

Although sentence starters or frames could be cloze questions that can test students' ability to recall and use a specific term or phrase (e.g., "The _____ of boys to girls is 3 to 2."), they can also reinforce production of key academic language or specific mathematical terms (e.g., *diagram*, *relationship*, *the amount of*) and/or focus students on key mathematical ideas (e.g., visual representations of quantities and relationships) so they can then use them in their own writing and speaking. Sentence Starters and Frames are also a tool for students' own mathematical thinking in order to learn about what students are thinking and prompt their further mathematical reasoning. For example, the sentence frame "I added . . . to the figure to show . . ." requires a creative response that encourages mathematical thinking about adding new features, such as auxiliary lines, to geometric visuals to help understand or solve a task.

---

[13] K. B. Chval and L. L. Khisty, "Latino Students, Writing, and Mathematics: A Case Study of Successful Teaching and Learning," in *Multilingualism in Mathematics Classrooms: Global Perspectives*, ed. R. Barwell (Clevedon, UK: Multilingual Matters, 2009) 128–144.

You should use a variety of sentence starters and frames that can accommodate a range of English proficiency levels. A sentence starter such as "A relationship I see is . . ." may be more challenging because it is more open ended and therefore more difficult to complete than others, such as "I see Raul's candies (in the diagram) . . ." In this sentence, the relationship is defined, and the student is asked to say where the quantity is in the diagram and can point or describe it. A sentence starter or frame crafted for students with lower English proficiency levels may provide opportunities to practice language while requiring that students complete the sentence using only a word or two. For students with higher English language proficiency levels, sentence starters or frames may include more sophisticated sentence structures or more challenging words and/or require longer responses. You can also allow students to choose from a list of sentence starters. For example, you could post and use a combination of the following sentence starters and sentence frames to structure the reflection but also allow student choice:

- I learned . . .

- It helped me when . . .

- I can change a geometric drawing by . . .

- Adding . . . to a geometric drawing can help me . . .

- The next time I have a geometry problem like this I will try . . . because . . .

The list of sentence starters and frames above include some that are more open-ended and allow for a wide range of student reflection, such as "I learned" and "It helped me when." Others are asking for more specific responses, for example, about how to change a diagram or how modifying a geometric drawing is helpful. Sentence starters that are more specific may be most appropriate when the objective is to assess student understanding of a vocabulary term or particular idea. In other cases, the more open sentence starters may not provide the detailed assessment information but allow for student reflection or formative assessment. To use sentence starters or frames, the teacher should anticipate or draft student responses, thinking critically about what students' responses could be and if a completed sentence would support language objectives and/or objectives to capture evidence of mathematical thinking. Finally, teachers should consider how and when they will help students make transitions from the use of a sentence starter or frame to constructing sentences on their own. One way to make this transition would be to use fewer words in a sentence starter, but ask students to use new vocabulary or specific terms in their writing. For example, a sentence starter that starts with, "The ratio between the two ticket sales is shown in the diagram by . . ." could become, "The ratio between . . ." where students are then asked to complete the sentence and reference the diagram.

## Co-constructed Word Bank

The Co-constructed Word Bank builds on the common idea of word banks or word walls (e.g., see Carr et al. 2009 for more information about word walls)[14] and includes phrases and terms related to the problem context or task as well as words and phrases that both students and teachers find important or raise during discussions about the problem.[15] Co-constructing the word bank by asking students for words or phrases that they feel are important, or aren't sure what they mean, can help teachers learn which words and phrases students are attending to or do not know. For example, when one teacher in our work was co-constructing a word bank with her students while introducing a task about the populations in two towns, she was surprised when students included the word *town*, and she realized that some of her students were not familiar with this word as they lived in a city.

Similar to other types of word banks, the Co-constructed Word Bank keeps important words in writing visible to students throughout a lesson so that they can study the words and attempt to use them in their speaking and writing and so the teacher can point students to those terms and phrases and encourage their use. In this manner, a Co-constructed Word Bank helps to support ELs' language production by providing them with access to mathematical language that they can use to communicate with others about the math task and their mathematical reasoning. When teachers ask students to use particular words or phrases from the Co-constructed Word Bank, they are prompting language production by all their students but especially the ELs. These practices provide access and opportunities to rich mathematical language for students of different English proficiency levels.

---

[14] J. Carr, C. Carroll, S. Cremer, M. Gale, R. Lagunoff, and U. Sexton, *Making Mathematics Accessible to English Learners: A Guidebook for Teachers* (San Francisco, CA: WestEd, 2009).

[15] J. W. Stigler, C. Fernandez, and M. Yoshida, "Traditions of School Mathematics in Japanese and American Elementary Classrooms," in *Theories of Mathematical Learning*, eds. L. P. Steffe, P. Nesher, P. Cobb, G. A. Goldin, and B. Greer (Mahwah, NJ: Lawrence Erlbaum Associates, 1996), 149–75.

**Implementation:** The Co-constructed Word Bank is usually generated during the launch of a problem as students bring up phrases and terms that are in the context of the problem and that they use in their discussion of the problem or during the reading of the problem (e.g., while engaging in the Three Reads strategy). During the launch or introduction, teachers can also highlight and clarify other terms or phrases that they determine in their planning will support students' understanding and communication. Teachers collect the words and phrases into a Co-constructed Word Bank and encourage students to reference it when they write individually and when they communicate in partner talk and full-group share. The teacher may highlight when students use words from the word bank by pointing them out. Here is an example of what a student's record of a word bank co-constructed for a geometry task may look like:

Word Bank
Base, height, triangle, dotted line, Arrows, rotate, rectangle

Depending on the task and the needs of the students in the class (e.g., their English proficiency levels), the teacher may choose to categorize the words that go into the Co-constructed Word Bank. For example, the teacher could list nouns and verbs in different places and call out the verbs as *action words*. Another way of distinguishing different types of words in the Co-constructed Word Bank, other than writing them in different locations, is to write them in different colors. For example, recall the How Many People? task:

---

### How Many People?

The population of the town of Medtown is three times the size of the population of the town of Carburg.

The *difference* in the number of people in the two towns is 2,184 people.

How many people live in Medtown and Carburg **combined**?

Create a diagram that helps you to solve the problem. Show your work.

---

When co-constructing word banks with students, our collaborating teachers found that students had questions about context words such as *town* and *population*, but the teacher and students also added comparison words and phrases that they thought would be useful such as *larger than* and *difference between*. The teacher could write these different types of words in different colors, for example, noting the words that are about the context of the task, ones that are action words, or ones that describe relating quantities, and discuss or highlight the types of words with students.

The Co-constructed Word Bank ties nicely with the Clarifying Vocabulary strategy, where teachers consider in advance the terms that should be discussed at some point in the lesson or terms that may need clarifying. It is also important to note that the Co-constructed Word Bank offers additional opportunities for students to share other terms that were new or that needed clarifying for their work on the task.

For example, the Co-constructed Word Bank can be a tool that helps students identify a word in the How Many People? task, which two of our project teachers, Meg and Sandra (not their real names), did not know would confuse students as they engaged with the task. Meg found that this strategy, in contrast with her self-made word bank, is one that helped her learn about her students.

Meg: I plan on using, creating our *own* word bank, which maybe I wouldn't have thought of before. I usually give them the word bank, and we talk about it briefly, but I don't think that it sinks in as much as "you tell me, what do we need to know?"

Sandra: First of all, when they said how many people in a town, in my class, nobody knew what a town was—

Meg: They live in a city—

Sandra: And if I'd created that word bank, I never would have put the word *town* in there. I just would have assumed.

Meg: I think that we make a lot of assumptions like that, but I think that [with the Co-constructed Word Bank], we are giving them the opportunity and the voice to make it themselves. (End-of-program focus group interview, June, 2013)

Both Sandra and Meg went on to describe how they saw value in the Co-constructed Word Bank because they had not identified the nonmathematical words that may hinder ELs' engagement with the task. In this manner, the co-constructed nature of the word bank supports ELs in engaging in the task and moving toward meeting language objectives as well.

Teachers should select when in the lesson they will encourage students to use words from the Co-constructed Word Bank and determine which words or phrases are important for all or some students to focus on (and then indicate those words by circling them or having students write them on their papers). To make these decisions about when to use this strategy, consider students' language ability as well as the language and mathematics objectives. For example, when the term *ratio* is in the task, a teacher who considers that this term may be new to students may choose to do the Co-constructed Word Bank immediately after students read the task or during the Three Reads strategy because a fragile understanding of *ratio* may prevent student engagement with the task and because the teacher would want students to use the term in conversation. Or, a teacher may choose to open class by introducing the Co-constructed Word Bank with the word *ratio* already in it, and share a definition for ratio while letting students know this is going to be an important word for the task. The teacher should then offer students opportunities to find additional words to include during the introduction to and work on the task; this use may encourage students to identify additional terms during the Three Reads of the task or to populate the Co-constructed Word Bank when working as pairs. Teachers can specify that students use certain words or a certain number of words during their discussion with peers or in group discussion.

## Pairs Work

ELs need as many opportunities to produce mathematical language and communication and share their ideas during the course of a mathematical lesson as possible, and during full-group interactions, the opportunities per student are limited. When working in pairs or small groups, all students, if supported as needed (e.g., with language access strategies when introducing the task or with sentence starters to help students talk with their partner), can have opportunities to talk about the mathematics. Furthermore, the opportunity to try out ideas with a partner and to hear what a partner has to say prior to a full-group sharing of ideas can build students' confidence to speak in the full group and give them needed practice in talking about the mathematics before expressing the same ideas in the full group.

**Implementation:** Before the lesson, consider what language access strategies need to be used to set up students to be able to work on the task so that they will be successful when moving to individual and pairs work. For example, you might choose to pair a student at a lower English language proficiency level with another student who speaks the same first language but has a slightly higher English language proficiency level. Then, consider what proportion of time should be allotted to individual time to begin making sense of the task, to pairs work on the task, and to full-group discussion of work on the task, as well as what supports students will need at each stage. Individual time prior to moving into pairs or small groups can allow students to start to develop their own mathematical ideas, which can then help fuel discussions in pairs or small groups. Sentence starters or questions can be helpful supports to guide the work in pairs or small groups when students move to working with peers. Don't assume that students need to complete the task while working in pairs or small groups before the sharing of ideas happens in the full group. A productive and engaging full-group discussion about the mathematics can happen based on partially formed ideas.

## Strategies That Address Both Language Access and Language Production

### Differentiated Teacher Questions

The Differentiated Teacher Questions strategy provides different levels of support through phrasing and word choice in order to offer students of different language levels appropriate and scaffolded opportunities for participation. For example, differentiating the question, "What is the combined population of Medtown and Carburg?" could mean modifying the question to support ELs who might be unfamiliar with the words *population* or *combined* and would benefit by having increased access to the mathematics if the word *population* were changed to *number of people* and *combined* were changed to *total*. Or, differentiating teacher questions could include the word *combined* as a new term but with clarification or addition to a Co-constructed Word Bank. Differentiated teacher questions can provide scaffolding for ELs within the questions themselves, to support student access to the question content, and should be written so an appropriate response includes targeted academic language. Differentiated teacher questions can be used during any part of a lesson, including the launch and partner-work time. Including targeted academic language in the question provides support to ELs by providing more opportunities to hear appropriate use of the language multiple times.

**Implementation:** Before the lesson, consider the ELs in your classroom and what parts of the lesson will include differentiated teacher questions.

Thinking of the specific English proficiency levels of students in the classroom and the academic language you want these specific students to produce, write questions so students at the target English proficiency level can understand the question and are likely to use the targeted academic vocabulary in their response. You can also combine questions with other types of language access support. The table below lists some language access support types that could be combined with a question, using examples specific to the How Many People? task shown earlier in this chapter:

| Language Access Support to Combine with a Teacher Question | Example |
|---|---|
| Modeling academic language | How does your diagram represent the quantity that is the population of Carburg? |
| Rephrasing | How many more people live in the bigger town? |
| Using alternate word(s) | How many people are in Medtown and Carburg **together**? |
| Using translated word(s) (in a student's first language) | What is the population of Medtown and Carburg *en total*? |
| Gesturing | How does this diagram show that the population of Medtown *(point at Medtown's population in the diagram)* is three times *(hold up three fingers)* the population of Carburg's *(point at Carburg's population in the diagram)*? |

Teachers can also turn questions into sentence starters or sentence frames for students to use in their work. For example, you may write or type these sentence starters and frames on small pieces of paper to give to students to use, perhaps in conjunction with asking those students the questions. You may also post the questions or the targeted academic language in the classroom during the class period or write specific, targeted questions on an individual student's assignment. Academic vocabulary that has been used before could also be referred to while you ask the question, such as underlining terms on a task handout, reminding students of an entry in a student vocabulary notebook, or pointing to words on a word wall.

Teachers may also differentiate questions by considering a student's English language proficiency (ELP) level and choose questions to ask students about their work based on their ELP levels. To differentiate by ELP level, consider using alternative words, rephrasing of questions, academic language, and gestures to support students' language access, as noted above. For example, possible questions for the Sharing Candies task are listed in the table below, clustered by ELP level. Questions for students with limited English language proficiency, for example beginning or early intermediate students, can involve more gesturing and fewer words. Students of higher English language proficiency may be more prepared for questions that initially use targeted vocabulary, such as quantities, or that have multiple parts.

| English Language Proficiency (ELP) Levels | Example of Differentiated Teacher Questions using Sharing Candies task |
|---|---|
| Beginning | • Point to/show me Raul's/Jasmine's/Sara's candies . . .<br>• Who has more candy? How does your diagram show that?<br>• What amount does this represent? |
| Emergent/Early Intermediate | • Where did you represent the candies that Sara had left?<br>• What fraction of the candies did Jasmine get? Raul? |
| Developing/ Intermediate | • Show how the quantities are related to each other in your diagram.<br>• How can you use your diagram to find out . . . "the answer to a question" or "how many candies Sara had to start"? |
| Bridging and Reaching | • What relationship do you see between the amount of candy Sara has at the end and the amount of candy she gave away?<br>• How does your diagram represent the amount of candy Raul has? Sara ended with? Sara started with? |

## Frayer Model

The Frayer Model as used in education builds off the early work by Dorothy Frayer and colleagues.[16] A Frayer Model is a graphic organizer that consists of a four-part frame within which you define the word, phrase, or concept, indicate its characteristics or facts about it, and provide examples and nonexamples. See the examples below of Frayer Models for the term *area*. Sometimes the target word or concept is written in an oval or box in the middle of the chart, or the model may include different attributes, such as essential and nonessential characteristics.

---

[16] D. A. Frayer, W. C. Frederick, and H. G. Klausmeier, *A Schema for Testing the Level of Concept Mastery*. Working paper No. 16 (Madison, WI: University of Wisconsin, 1969).

## Area

| Definition | Facts |
|---|---|
| space inside a 2-D shape number of square units inside | measure in square units (units$^2$ or in.$^2$) 2-D objects like squares, circles |
| **Examples** painted wall  floor tiles garden <br><br> ← 6 square units | **Nonexamples** border  perimeter <br><br> fencing to go around  length neighborhood (not in math class!) |

Using a Frayer Model can support ELs by organizing learning of a new term or concept into separate, small steps. The model focuses on different elements of a term, such as the definition, and then pairs them with examples, highlighting different understandings of a word that are helpful to know for mathematical work and allowing students to focus on each concept or box within the model at his or her own pace. A Frayer Model can help students build understanding by activating and categorizing prior knowledge and making connections between terms and concepts through contrasting examples with nonexamples. It can structure clarifying discussions that go beyond simply providing definitions, as teacher(s) and students share, compare, and possibly negotiate responses as they collaboratively create meaning. Make sure that examples and nonexamples help move students' mathematical thinking forward by using mathematical context or other mathematical terms, as necessary. In this manner, nonexamples should give insight into the examples; for example, fencing is a nonexample of area because it is the edge and not the inside of a yard, and students sometimes confuse perimeter and area. In contrast, a pair of glasses is not an example of area, but it is not a productive nonexample because it does not support a students' thinking about area at all!

**Implementation:** Frayer Models can be used during the sense-making part or launch of a mathematics task as a way to understand the mathematical vocabulary in a task or context. Students can work on them individually and in pairs, then the teacher can lead a whole-class discussion asking students to share their own or their partner's responses. Sentence starters or frames can be used in conjunction with Frayer Models to help students share responses, for example, "A nonexample of *area* is . . .

because . . ." If Frayer Models are used regularly, a set of completed models can act as a reference.

| **Frayer Model for** _____ | |
|---|---|
| **Definition** | **Facts** |
| **Examples** | **Nonexamples** |

## Teacher Revoicing

Revoicing, a strategy discussed often in the context of language instruction embedded in content instruction (e.g., Lyster 2007),[17] involves listening closely to student thinking and then rephrasing and revoicing student ideas, inserting mathematical vocabulary, asking students for clarity, and/or making suggestions of the relations between students' ideas to other strategies or vocabulary. By revoicing, teachers support student academic language production while relating the mathematical talk to the students' own ideas.[18] To use revoicing most effectively, teachers should attend closely to students' ideas and then differentiate their response based on student language proficiency levels.[19]

---

[17] R. Lyster, *Learning and Teaching Languages Through Content: A Counterbalanced Approach* (Amsterdam/Philadelphia: John Benjamins, 2007).

[18] J. Moschkovich, "A Situated and Sociocultural Perspective on Bilingual Mathematics Learners," *Mathematical Thinking & Learning* 4, nos. 2 and 3 (2002): 189–212.

[19] K. B. Chval and O. Chávez, "Designing Math Lessons for English Language Learners," *Mathematics Teaching in the Middle School* 17, no. 5 (2011): 261–65.

**Implementation:** Revoicing is an opportunity to highlight key academic language and orient students to key mathematical ideas. Revoicing can be used throughout a lesson; for example, this strategy can clarify terms and students' ideas during the beginning of a lesson when students share responses during the Three Reads strategy, and it can be used when students are sharing their work during full-group discussions. While revoicing, think critically about when and how to insert certain vocabulary, listening closely to students' own understanding to build on what students are saying and being mindful of student English proficiency levels. Timing is important. If a student is in the middle of solving a task, revoicing may not be helpful, as the student is concentrating on the solution (Lyster 2007).[17] However, if a student is looking back and describing a solution process, then revoicing may help him or her bring precision to the explanation. It is also important to recognize the terms that may have multiple meanings or a meaning specific to mathematics and discuss the meaning as it relates to the task. To avoid confusion, introduce only new academic vocabulary terms that are connected to the students' ideas. In a geometry context, revoicing could be used when students are discussing figures (e.g., a parallelogram), possibly by including the specific relevant vocabulary (e.g., *parallelogram*, *side*, *vertex*, *parallel*, *quadrilateral*), which would support students describing the figure and its properties or any related transformations more accurately. The aim of Revoicing is to build on students' ideas in a manner that supports increasingly precise student communication (rather than evaluating or correcting student vocabulary usage). For example, listen carefully to students' informal use of math terms, such as *flipping* a triangle or *the straight line*, and then revoice by introducing and supporting students' use of more formal math terms, such as *rotate* or *perpendicular*. It is important to introduce terms that connect to students' own ideas in order to build on and not dismiss student reasoning; for example, *straight* is a term often used by middle graders, having several different meanings. You would want to listen to how the student is describing a line as *straight* to determine the most appropriate academic vocabulary to use when you revoice the idea. In this example, Revoicing may be using the term *parallel* if the student is discussing two lines in the same plane, or the term *perpendicular* if lines intersect at a right angle, or the teacher may need to engage in gesturing when clarifying words to support student associations and understanding. The Teacher Revoicing strategy can be used with the Co-constructed Word bank to make connections between student and teacher ideas and the target vocabulary. This strategy can be implemented across a task, including when students are reading the task, discussing the task with a partner, or sharing the relationships identified during a full-group discussion. Similar to the Clarifying Vocabulary strategy, it is critical to note the language goals and targeted language in order to support student language access and production through making connections between concepts, informal language, and targeted language concurrently.

# Choosing Strategies for Your Class

In this chapter we have presented a wide variety of instructional strategies to be integrated into mathematics classrooms. Not all strategies should be used all the time, and strategies should be implemented in ways that take into consideration the students they are intended to support. Therefore, an important question is how to select among strategies for a given lesson or group of students. We provided some guidance about implementation within our description of each strategy, but here are some general questions and ideas to keep in mind when planning the use of these instructional strategies:

- **What is your goal in using the strategy, or what challenge are you trying to address by using it?** If you are trying to ensure students understand enough of the language of the task or lesson to be able to engage in productive struggle around the mathematics, a strategy that really targets language access is important, e.g., Three Reads or Clarifying Vocabulary. If you are trying to support students to share their mathematical thinking with others, then a production-focused strategy is important, e.g., Sentence Starters or targeting particular vocabulary from a Co-constructed Word Bank. You may also consider whether your primary goals during the planned lesson relate to supporting speaking or writing (in the case of language production) and to reading or listening (in the case of language access). Considering the mode of communication will be important to decisions about how to tailor the strategy, e.g., how many of the reads in the Three Reads to do aloud and when to show the text of the task to the students for the reads.

- **How do you know which students need this strategy (or a differentiated form of this strategy)?** Perhaps you will use Acting Out of the task context for the whole class, or perhaps you will do it with small groups who you determine during the flow of the lesson are confused about the task context. Consider the data you have about what the students in this class need to get started on this task, and be careful not to make assumptions that students understand something because they do not ask a question or because some of their classmates understand it, or that they don't understand and need the additional support. Students' ELP levels can provide information about their language needs, but it is also important to listen to student participation and look carefully at each assignment for insight into a student's language use in class.

- **How does this strategy fit into the timing and flow of the lesson I am planning?** For example, the Frayer Model and the Three Reads strategy are both important and beneficial strategies, but they each take some time, and a lesson needs to be planned accordingly to accommodate them (and perhaps both would not fit in the same lesson!). On other hand, sentence starters and sentence frames can be integrated into pairs or full-group discussions already included in a given lesson.

- **How do I use the strategies for the different ELP levels of the students whom I am looking to support?** For example, sentence starters can be tailored to the English language proficiency level of students by attending to the complexity of sentence construction. The sentence starter *Diagrams show . . .* is simple phrasing, involving a subject and a present tense verb. *An important characteristic of a useful diagram is . . . because . . .* is a more complex language construction with a causal statement involved. Of course, these two particular examples also get at different mathematical ideas about diagrams. Some of our collaborating teachers determined that when they asked their students with beginner levels of English language proficiency carefully constructed questions, the students were able to express their mathematical thinking orally. In addition, some students who had slightly higher ELP levels could transition from the questions to some similar sentence starters. In this manner, differentiated questions may support the use of differentiated sentence starters. Another example of tailoring strategies based on the English language proficiency level of students is in the selection of words or phrases from a Co-constructed Word Bank to require or encourage students to use during their work on the task.

You might assign different words to different students to use during their partner discussion or during full-group sharing based on their English language proficiency levels. Other examples of differentiating the strategies based on English language proficiency are found in the descriptions of the strategies earlier.

- **What mode of communication am I working to support for students?** Students need many opportunities to read, write, speak, and listen during mathematical work. Most strategies can be used whether the primary mode is writing or speaking, but it is important to make planned choices about when to have students work with written text versus oral speech.

## Conclusion

To support their learning of both mathematics and language, all ELs need regular opportunities to describe their mathematical thinking, detail their solution processes, and present their arguments and conclusions both orally and in writing.[20] That is, supporting communication and developing language needs to be situated *in the context of mathematical work.* The research-based instructional strategies in this chapter follow this goal by tying together mathematics learning objectives and the overall goal to support students' mathematical thinking and communication. Productive and proficient mathematical communication is more than academic language and vocabulary but includes sharing mathematical thinking, critiquing the reasoning of others, and participating in other discursive practices within the mathematics class. Therefore, in order to focus on language and communication in mathematics, the strategies set the stage for integrating language, mathematics, and general communication goals, and then the teacher must also engage in modifying the strategies to meet students' needs and the task demands and to meet the mathematics objectives of the lesson.

---

[20] J. Moschkovich, "Supporting the Participation of English Language Learners in Mathematical Discussions," *For the Learning of Mathematics* 19, no. 1 (1999): 11–19.

# Chapter 5

# Designing Tasks to Support Access for English Learners

Mathematics tasks come in a variety of forms, including:

- Tasks meant to prompt recall of facts or prompt practice of learned procedures

- Tasks meant to prompt application of learned procedures in situations that also require some reasoning about the structure of the procedures (for example, think of what is required to find two different sets of six numbers, each set with mean equal to 42)

- Problem-solving/reasoning tasks where paths to solutions are not immediately clear, and where solutions often require more than direct applications of known procedures

Most, if not all, curricula used in schools have a mix of all these. Each type is suited to its purpose, whether that purpose is knowledge recall, skill reinforcement, or application of knowledge and skill in problem solving and reasoning situations. In this book, we have focused on the third category of tasks. That category is richest in opportunities to include visual representations and use of mathematical communication and reasoning, as well as opportunities to collect informative records of student thinking—all for the purpose of providing mathematics access for ELs.

# Task Design Principles

While the texture and depth of tasks can shift dramatically, depending on purpose, there are some common task features to concentrate on, which we have distilled into six design principles. We do not insist that every task be true to all six design principles, but we have learned that, over time, we do well to pay heed to all of them. This seems especially true when an over-arching purpose is—as it is in this book—to increase access for English learners to mathematical thinking and communication.

1. *The Content Principle.* Does the problem involve concepts or procedures that are recognizably connected to content and mathematical practice standards for the different grades? Will you and your students see the relevance of the content to classroom work?

2. *The Evidence of Thinking Principle.* Will the response require students to think, beyond mere application of procedures, and to reveal their thinking about the task?

3. *The Wide Access Principle.* Will all students, including those who typically struggle in mathematics, find productive as well as engaging ways to enter the problem?

4. *The Multimodal Principle.* Does the problem invite visual, e.g., diagrammatic, approaches? Does it prompt verbal or written explanations? Will opportunities arise for teachers to help students develop and reinforce effective communication and academic language?

5. *The Closure Principle.* Will students (and their teachers) find adequate and appropriate ways to terminate their work on the problem—perhaps not the same closure for all?

6. *The Extension-Generalization Principle.* Will the procedures, explanations, constructions, conjectures, and so on produced by the students apply to other situations?

Attention to these principles can help shape tasks to meet your instructional needs, especially where those needs involve helping ELs become more mathematically proficient. Below are two examples, drawn from two topics that are familiar to all middle school students and their teachers: fractions and area.

## Example 1: Fractions

### Content Principle

We start by considering the aspects of fractions that make them so important and relevant to student success. For one, proficiency with fractions is an essential prerequisite for success in mathematics topics that are featured in, then extend beyond, middle grades. More specifically, for students to succeed in algebra, they must understand that fractions serve as more than representations of parts of wholes, that they also represent numbers with *magnitude*.[1] What does a task look like that builds knowledge and skills in using fractions as numbers with magnitude? Think about the kinds of tasks we give younger students to see if they understand magnitude in whole numbers. We might want to know if they can successfully compare two ("Which is larger, 340 or 430?"); in addition, we might want to know if they have a sense of the relative magnitudes ("What is a whole number that is between 340 and 430?"). We can do the same with fractions, so let's take the following as a task starting point:

*Which is the larger number, $4/7$ or $4/5$?*

*Find a fraction between $4/7$ and $4/5$.*

### Evidence of Thinking Principle

By "evidence of thinking," we mean any record students leave and/or make accessible later to themselves, to other learners, and to teachers. Records can benefit the learners themselves because their presence can lighten cognitive load that would build quickly toward overload if the mind had to keep it all internalized. Records can also enlighten other learners because they can be used to piece together a narrative of thinking about a task, as well as give them new ways to think about their own work. For teachers, records of thinking can guide formative assessment and instructional interventions, which can be invaluable to teachers of English learners.

---

[1]  M. Schneider and R. S. Siegler, "Representations of the Magnitudes of Fractions," *Journal of Experimental Psychology: Human Perception and Performance* 36, no. 5 (2010): 1227–38.

In order to gauge student mathematical thinking, we need records of what students *did*, of course, but also records of the thinking behind what they chose to do. While sometimes such records can be spoken, usually it is most convenient to seek written records of thinking. In the end, there should be a variety of thinking apparent across students. Otherwise, if student responses look alike, then the task may not be challenging enough, or, in some cases, the teacher's prompts were too leading. Variety in students' thinking is valuable.

Some students might think, "$4/7$ is smaller than $4/5$ because $1/7$ is smaller than $1/5$ and so 4 of the $1/7$s is smaller than 4 of the $1/5$s. To find a fraction between them, take 6, a number between 5 and 7, and so $4/6$ is between $4/7$ and $4/5$." This method applies directly to similar pairs like $5/6$ and $5/8$, but for $8/9$ and $8/10$, there is no whole number between 9 and 10. Many students in middle grades will try $8/9.5$ and see this is equivalent to $16/19$, which is a fraction between $8/9$ and $8/10$. So, the method continues to work for them, and they have found "regularity in repeated reasoning," which is the core of Mathematical Practice 8, *Look for and express regularity in repeated reasoning*.

Other students might approach the problem visually, for example, making use of the geometric structure of the number line, consistent with Mathematical Practice 7, *Look for and make use of structure*.

To capture all such examples of student thinking, in student written narrative, we might prompt the records as follows:

*Which is the larger number, $4/7$ or $4/5$? Explain your thinking.*

*Find a fraction between $4/7$ and $4/5$. Explain your thinking.*

## Wide Access Principle

For all students, but especially English learners, a fundamental consideration for access to a task is the wording of the task. Are there too many words? Are there words that may be unfamiliar, particularly to students whose first language is not English? These considerations relate to access to understanding the task. On brief examination, it appears that our wording is brief enough and familiar enough. However, another aspect of access relates to how well students are enabled to proceed with what we have prompted them to do. In our case, we have prompted written explanation. For ELs with low English proficiency, this may be difficult. So, we can incorporate sentence frames:

*Which is the larger number, ⁴/₇ or ⁴/₅? Explain your thinking: I know that ___ is a larger number than ___ because _____.*

*Find a fraction between ⁴/₇ and ⁴/₅. Explain your thinking: The number ___ is between ⁴/₇ and ⁴/₅ because _____.*

We try, in offering tasks for ELs, to balance the prompts for verbal explanations with opportunities, if not direct prompts, to use visual representations of their thinking, which we take up next.

## Multimodal Principle

We have already invoked the multimodal principle in asking for students to write explanations. With English learners, it often is important to expand the modes further by inviting or requiring the use of visual representations of thinking. So, we might have:

*Which is the larger number, ⁴/₇ or ⁴/₅? Show your thinking on the number line. Then explain your thinking by completing this sentence: My number line shows that ___ is a larger number than ___ because _____.*

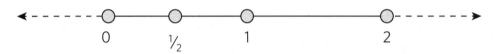

*Find a fraction between ⁴/₇ and ⁴/₅. Show your thinking on the number line. Explain your thinking by completing this sentence: My number line shows that ___ is between ⁴/₇ and ⁴/₅ because _____.*

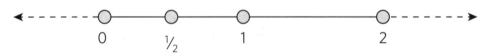

We also have found it valuable to have students work in pairs on tasks, and we incorporate a prompt to "explain to your partner what you did" before they write explanations. This expands the number of modes even further—combining oral explanation with written explanation and visual representation.

## Levels of Closure Principle

For some more open-ended tasks, recognizing when one is at a point of closure can be challenging. (See Example 2, below, for a case.) However, in this fraction task, the closure boundaries are pretty clear. Some students respond to the first part, describing their thinking on comparing the two fractions, but do not know how to find a fraction between the two. In principle (though less likely), students might be able to complete the second part and not the first. Others respond to both fraction tasks, then follow the prompts to explain the thinking behind the responses. So, in this particular case, we have adhered to the principle rather closely.

### Extension-Generalization Principle

When invoked, this principle often connects to Mathematical Practice 8, *Look for and express regularity in repeated reasoning.* It is not necessary that each task contain this component (for one thing, it is time-consuming), but because generalizing is an important mathematical process, it is valuable to engage students occasionally in exploring how far their strategies can apply. One way to do this is to ask them, as a last step in the task, to try out their strategies with similar pairs of numbers:

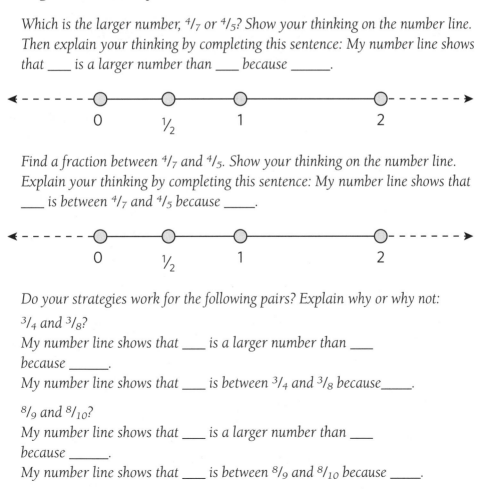

*Which is the larger number, $4/7$ or $4/5$? Show your thinking on the number line. Then explain your thinking by completing this sentence: My number line shows that ____ is a larger number than ____ because _____.*

*Find a fraction between $4/7$ and $4/5$. Show your thinking on the number line. Explain your thinking by completing this sentence: My number line shows that ____ is between $4/7$ and $4/5$ because _____.*

*Do your strategies work for the following pairs? Explain why or why not:*
*$3/4$ and $3/8$?*
*My number line shows that ____ is a larger number than ____ because _____.*
*My number line shows that ____ is between $3/4$ and $3/8$ because_____.*

*$8/9$ and $8/10$?*
*My number line shows that ____ is a larger number than ____ because _____.*
*My number line shows that ____ is between $8/9$ and $8/10$ because _____.*

What about $^{100}/_{101}$ and $^{100}/_{105}$?

___ is a larger number than ___ because _____.

___ is between $^{100}/_{101}$ and $^{100}/_{105}$ because ____.

## Example 2: Area

### Content Principle

In our experience, when middle-grade students approach area tasks, many resort quickly to applying formulas. This is not surprising, because much of their prior experience with school mathematics has involved computational procedures of one sort or another. Of course, mathematics is much more than number crunching, so students should learn when use of formulas is appropriate, and when it is not. Tasks can help in that regard.

Area is about space and measurement; numbers and formulas are means to connect space and measurement. How might a task elicit thinking about space and measurement as features of a geometric figure's area? In other words, how can a task forestall the rush to formula use? One technique that often can succeed is to set up a task that works "backward," in the sense that it starts with the result—in this case, the area—and asks questions about starting conditions. This is emblematic of the algebraic habit of mind doing-undoing, described in *Fostering Algebraic Thinking*,[2] in that we ask students to start at the end, and "undo" to reveal the steps that produced the end. For example, here is a basic task (drawn from *Fostering Geometric Thinking*):[3]

> Two vertices of a triangle are located at (0,4) and (0,10). The area of the triangle is 12 units². Find a third vertex that, with (0,4) and (0,10), makes a triangle of area 12 units². Explain how you found the third vertex.
>
> Now find a different vertex that also forms, with (0,4) and (0,10), a triangle of area 12 units². Explain how you found this different vertex.

---

[2] M. Driscoll, *Fostering Algebraic Thinking* (Portsmouth, NH: Heinemann, 1999).
[3] M. Driscoll et al., *Fostering Geometric Thinking* (Portsmouth, NH: Heinemann, 2007).

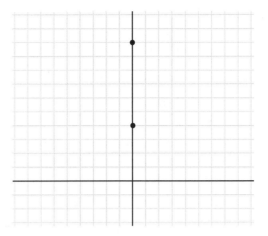

## Evidence of Thinking Principle

In our experience with this area task, many students find a right triangle (say, by trying (4,4) as the third vertex), then reflect it across the y-axis to locate a second vertex that works. That reflects productive, though limited, thinking—limited, because right triangles are so familiar to middle graders. Prompts that push students toward the unfamiliar can enrich the thinking and so also the records of thinking:

> *Two vertices of a triangle are located at (0,4) and (0,10). The area of the triangle is 12 units². Find a third vertex that, with (0,4) and (0,10), makes a triangle of area 12 units². Explain how you found the third vertex.*
>
> *Now find a different vertex that also forms, with (0,4) and (0,10), a triangle of area 12 units². Explain how you found this different vertex.*
>
> *Find more vertices that work, and answer these questions:*
>
> > *a) How many right triangles are there that work? List the coordinates of the third vertex for each of the right triangles. Explain how you know you have found all the right triangles that work.*
> >
> > *b) How many isosceles triangles are there that work? List the coordinates of the third vertex for each of the isosceles triangles. Explain how you know they are isosceles triangles. Explain how you know you have found all the isosceles triangles that work.*
> >
> > *c) Find a different triangle that works (not a right triangle and not an isosceles triangle). Explain how you found this new vertex.*

## The Wide Access Principle

This task is wordier than the fractions task in Example 1, which suggests this task, when implemented in the classroom, might benefit from including the Three Reads strategy described in Chapter 4. Furthermore, there are geometric terms like *units²*, *vertex*, *right triangle*, *coordinates*, and *isosceles triangle*, which suggests the implementation might also benefit from teachers and students developing a Co-constructed Word Bank, also described in Chapter 4. Finally, we can also incorporate Sentence Starters and Frames to widen access to written explanations.

> *Two vertices of a triangle are located at (0,4) and (0,10). The area of the triangle is 12 units². Find a third vertex that, with (0,4) and (0,10), makes a triangle of area 12 units². Complete the sentences: The new vertex I found is____. I found the third vertex by _____.*
>
> *Now find a different vertex that also forms, with (0,4) and (0,10), a triangle of area 12 units². Complete: The new vertex I found is____. I found this new vertex by_____.*
>
> *Find more vertices that work, and answer:*
>
> > *a) How many right triangles are there that work? I found ____ right triangles that work. The coordinates of the new third vertices are_____. I know I have found all the right triangles that work because _____.*
> >
> > *b) How many isosceles triangles are there? I found ____ isosceles triangles that work. The coordinates of the new third vertices are _____. I know I have found all the isosceles triangles that work because _____.*
> >
> > *c) Find a different triangle that works (not a right triangle and not an isosceles triangle). The new vertex I found is_____. I found this new vertex by_____.*

## Multimodal Principle

As in Example 1, the prompts for students to write explanations, and to do so using academic terms like *coordinates*, are consistent with the multimodal principle. As for adding visual representations to complement the writing, perhaps you already recognize that an advantage of geometric/spatial reasoning tasks, such as this Area 12 task, is that the visual representation is part of the task presentation. Because a good part of student engagement on this task involves exploration, we have found it valuable to make sure that students have multiple copies of the grid to explore on.

## Levels of Closure Principle

The task tries to build up from very familiar cases (right triangles) to less familiar cases (isosceles triangles) and then to perhaps even less familiar cases (obtuse triangles). This kind of layering in a problem where there are many correct answers can help students find their own exit levels, when they have perhaps exhausted their prior knowledge. In this case, many students do not see this obtuse triangle as having area 12 units$^2$ because they continue to believe that a triangle's altitude must lie within the triangle. For those students, and likely for other students, a group analysis of student solutions, led by the teacher, is important to deepen and consolidate students' understanding of the concept of triangle area.

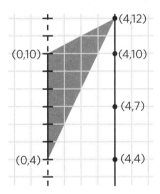

## Extension-Generalization Principle

An infinite number of points "work" to make area 12 units$^2$ triangles with (0,4) and (0,10) as the other two vertices. (Those points are all the points on the vertical lines $x = 4$ and $x = -4$.) When prompted to describe the set of points that "work" as third vertices, some students can grasp and describe this infinity of points. Many do not seem able to, but they can reason out that "there are more points that work." We have seen some middle graders conclude that all the points on the segment from (4,4) to (4,10) work, while others extend this, reasoning by symmetry that all the points on the segment from (−4, 4) to (−4,10) also work. These students may not be sure about the obtuse triangles, but they have worked toward extending/generalizing, and that is the point of this principle: to prompt reasoning that extends and generalizes. This prompt might look like the following, added at the end of the first parts of the Area 12 problem:

> d) *In addition to the points you have found, what other positions for the third vertex work? Complete: Points at _____ can also be the third vertex. I know they form triangles with (0,4) and (0,10) that have an area of 12 units² because_____.*

## Reflecting on These Examples

Examples 1 and 2 demonstrate the results of some of the conversations, both internal and external (among colleagues), we have had in order to shape two of the tasks for use with groups including EL students. The six task design principles guided the conversations. As you review tasks from your curricula, with an eye toward maximizing access for ELs, you can have similar conversations, both internal and external. In doing so, you may identify ways you can tweak a task to increase its EL access potential. Recall some of the highlights from Examples 1 and 2:

- *Put a premium on content that has high payoff for students.* For example, helping middle grade students become proficient with fractions as numbers with magnitude pays off in fractions computation and, later, in algebra. Similarly, proficiency with fractions in equipartitioning situations (also called fair sharing) is foundational to ratio-proportion knowledge and skills. (As an example, skill in equipartitioning allows someone to answer both of the following correctly: 1. If three people share seven pizzas, how much pizza does each person get? 2. If seven people share three pizzas, how much pizza does each person get?) In geometry, properties of figures, and relationships between figures are important mathematically; in word problems, emphasize understanding quantities and relationships among quantities. And so on.

- *Change the occasional task to become an undoing task.* If students can find the area of familiar figures, give them the area and have them determine figures that fit. If students know how to compute a mean, give them the mean and have them determine distributions whose numbers produce that mean. And so on.

- *When a task has a few or more correct answers, layer the prompts so that students have access up front and can successfully exit when they reach their limit.*

- *With EL students in mind, look for places to increase access to tasks using language strategies.* If a task seems wordy, consider using the Three Reads strategy. If there are words in a task that may be unfamiliar, consider using a Co-constructed Word Bank. Don't hesitate to incorporate writing in tasks, but consider prompting the writing with Sentence Starters and Frames. (See Chapter 4 for more information.)

# Important Language Features in Tasks

At times, it may seem that language plays a small role in mathematics and, by extension, in the teaching of mathematics. This is mainly an illusion, given force by the prevalence of abstract and often specialized symbols in mathematical work. In reality, language not only informs how we make sense for ourselves of these symbols and of ways they are used in mathematics but also how we as mathematics educators help students to make sense of them. The demands of teaching mathematics to English learners only magnify the role of language, as well as the risks in our not paying heed to language use.

With ELs in mind, task developers and task choosers must bear in mind the various ways in which language used in tasks can unintentionally limit access. Below is a list of language features we have found important to attend to in task development:

1.  Keep in mind that enhancing access to language in mathematics tasks and lessons does not require watering down the cognitive challenge in mathematics tasks for English learners. English proficiency is not a prerequisite for mathematical proficiency. Rather, you can employ ways for English learners to become proficient in language *while doing challenging mathematical work*, for example, by making use of language access and production strategies, along with mathematical visual representations, embedded in the mathematical tasks.

2.  Pay attention to how many words in a reading passage (e.g., in the text of a word problem) are *likely to be known* to all who will be reading it (e.g., the students, especially ELs, who will be expected to understand

the passage). A high percentage of the words should be familiar to readers—some experts estimate as much as 90 percent.

3.  When judging a passage for its accessibility, look for words that have multiple meanings (the linguistic term for this is *polysemy*)—for example, *fair*, which has one meaning in "fair sharing" and another in "county fair"; *left*, which can mean the remainder after a quantity has diminished, or it can indicate a spatial direction; and, as a third example, *product*, which can mean something that is purchased in a store or the result of multiplying two or more numbers together. We are not recommending that you avoid such words, but instead that you anticipate the challenges they may present for student understanding, and that you are explicit in helping students determine how they should interpret the use of such words in a particular context.

4.  Similarly, watch out for words and phrases drawn from contexts unfamiliar to English learners. Martiniello[4] gives a pointed example in the use of the word *chores* in an item on a state mathematics exam. It was an item on which ELs did particularly poorly, and she hypothesized that they did poorly on the item because *chores* was not a word English learners would hear used in English in non-English-speaking households, nor in their classrooms, nor in schoolyard interactions with their fellow students. You can think of this as the "schoolyard" criterion.

5.  Also, be alert for words that may be misheard by English learners. There are words, like *loose* and *lose*, that mean very different things in English but can sound similar. We recall an English learner, new to the country, hearing a task read out loud, including the clause "$3/_7$ of the apples were red." This clause also was written on the board as an "important piece of information." When the students were prompted to solve the task, the first thing this student did, as we observed, was draw a tree and carefully place 37 red dots on it: 37 red apples. Apparently, "three-sevenths" was heard as "three seven."

6.  Be especially sensitive to how mathematical ideas are expressed. Like other academic disciplines, mathematics has its own "register"—its own ways of employing language to construct and communicate

---

4  M. Martiniello, "Language and the Performance of English-Language Learners in Math Word Problems," *Harvard Educational Review* 78, no. 2 (2008): 333–68.

knowledge. Features of the mathematics register include technical vocabulary (e.g., "hypotenuse"), dense noun phrases (e.g., from Schleppegrell[5] [2007, 143] "the volume of a rectangular prism with sides 8, 10, and 12 cm"), precise definitions, and special norms for convincing argument. Some words have privileged meanings in mathematics, which may not transfer to nonmathematical contexts. For example, *any* often means "every" in mathematics, as in "Will your method work to change any parallelogram into a rectangle?" However, in everyday English, *any* can mean "some," as in "Do you have any idea?" "I don't have any money." Similarly, the phrase *some number* may be used to mean the same as "every number," or it may be used to imply a particular, but unknown, number, as in "some number is twice 4 plus 6." The overarching message here is: When writing or selecting a word problem, or when preparing a verbal explanation, take a few seconds to ask yourself, "Where are possible words that may cause difficulty or misinterpretation?"

7. Consider the length of passages and of sentences within passages. Often, the longer a sentence or passage is, the harder it is to follow the flow of ideas. If you note a long sentence or passage (e.g., in a word problem), and you have the option, break it into shorter sentences.

8. Be aware of how a task statement makes use of clauses. For example, if there are clauses within clauses, English learners may have difficulty. Conditional clauses—e.g., "if . . . then" constructions—also can be difficult to interpret, especially for English learners. We have seen cases where some English learners interpret a clause like "If the area of the rectangle is 60 square units . . ." as meaning that the area of the rectangle is not 60 square units. Again, our purpose in laying out this warning flag is not to tell you to avoid such clauses. Indeed, conditional clauses are essential to effective mathematical and scientific communication. We want you to be aware of the difficulties so you can help students to interpret the uses of clauses appropriately.

9. When you can, ask a colleague who is an ESL specialist to help you become more attuned to language issues. This can be done in occasional brief interactions. He or she might suggest rewordings of mathematics

---

[5] M. J. Schleppegrell, "The Linguistic Challenges of Mathematics Teaching and Learning: A Research Review," *Reading & Writing Quarterly* 23 (2007): 139–59.

tasks, help you analyze student work samples for evidence of language difficulty, and so on.

We find it is very helpful for mathematics educators to develop habits of mind that pay attention to aspects of language in planning mathematics tasks and lessons, and in teaching mathematics to English learners—vocabulary, sentence structure, density of ideas, and so on. For example, one can make a habit of looking at tasks and reflecting on such questions as *Are there too many words in this? What words or phrases may confuse? What words here have special meanings in mathematics?* Such habits of mind can benefit teachers by slowing them down a bit, so they might take time to consider alerts like, "I should reread that task statement to see what might be confusing, particularly to my students with low English language proficiency." Language-aware habits can enhance teachers' capacity to help students draw meaning from their interactions in mathematics lessons.

Last, remember that, with appropriate support, English learners at all English proficiency levels can practice regularly their use of written and spoken academic language in mathematics. Recall from Chapter 3 this example of student work on the Estella task. The student was at a beginning English proficiency level but made good use of the Co-constructed Word Bank and the Sentence Starters.

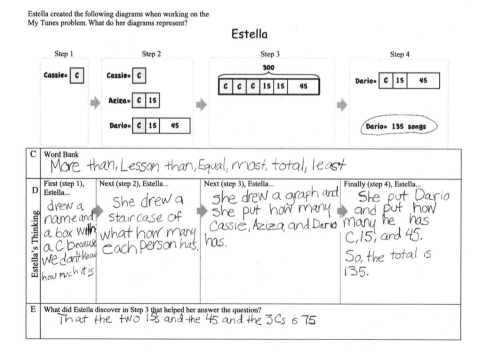

Estella created the following diagrams when working on the My Tunes problem. What do her diagrams represent?

**Estella**

| Step 1 | Step 2 | Step 3 | Step 4 |
|---|---|---|---|

Step 1: Cassie= C

Step 2: Cassie= C, Aziza= C 15, Dario= C 15 45

Step 3: 300 — C C C 15 15 45

Step 4: Dario= C 15 45, Dario= 135 songs

**C** Word Bank
More than, Lesson than, Equal, most, total, least

**Estella's Thinking**

**D**

First (step 1), Estella... drew a name and a box with a C because we don't know how much it is

Next (step 2), Estella... She drew a staircase of what how many each person has.

Next (step 3), Estella... she drew a graph and she put how many Cassie, Aziza, and Dario has.

Finally (step 4), Estella... She put Dario and put how many he has C, 15, and 45. So, the total is 135.

**E** What did Estella discover in Step 3 that helped her answer the question?
That the two 15s and the 45 and the 3 Cs is 75

# Visual Representations in Task Design

As we have seen, another critical piece of mastering mathematical communication, especially for English learners, is the use of *mathematical visual representations*. Chapter 2 addressed this in depth, but there are two considerations related specifically to task design: connecting visuals to the type of task, and making visual representations a habit.

## Connecting Visuals to Task Type

Mathematics contains more than a few visual representations: geometric drawings, Cartesian graphs, function tables, circle diagrams, tape diagrams, number lines, tree diagrams, flow charts, and so on. Some are better than others for representing different mathematical contexts. For example, tree diagrams are generally very helpful in probability problems; tables can help represent ratio and proportion tasks, as can double number lines and strip diagrams. Following is a chart matching types of visual representations with various quantitative and number tasks, with examples. The set is not intended to be comprehensive. We do not, for example, include tree diagrams or function tables here. For other such resources, check Sybilla Beckmann's book, *Mathematics for Elementary Teachers with Activity Manual, Third edition* (Boston, MA: Pearson Education, Inc., 2011), and also the website: http://dwwlibrary.wested.org/media/connecting-visuals-to-problem-types.

| Diagram Types | Task Types | Example Tasks | Possible Visuals |
|---|---|---|---|
| Number lines | **Fraction magnitude problems** | Find a fraction that is between $3/4$ and $5/6$ | |
| | **Fraction change problems (unknown start)** | Clarisse spent $2/5$ of her money on a coat. She spent $1/3$ of what was left on shoes. She had $150 left. How much did she start with? | |

*Continued*

| Diagram Types | Task Types | Example Tasks | Possible Visuals |
|---|---|---|---|
| *Double number lines* | **Rates/Ratios** | Shawna used to spend $2/3$ of an hour driving to her job. Now that her job has moved 6 miles farther from her home, she spends $5/6$ of an hour driving to work at the same speed. How far is her job from her home? | |
| | **Percent (percent is a type of rate)** | Manuel bought a new jacket, paying 70% of the original price. Manuel paid $140. What was the original price? | |
| *Arrays* | **Fraction word problems** | Sara had a bag of candies. She gave $1/3$ of the candies to Raul. Then Sara gave $1/4$ of the candies she had left to Jasmine. After giving candies to Raul and Jasmine, Sara had 24 candies left in her bag. How many candies did Sara have at the beginning? | |

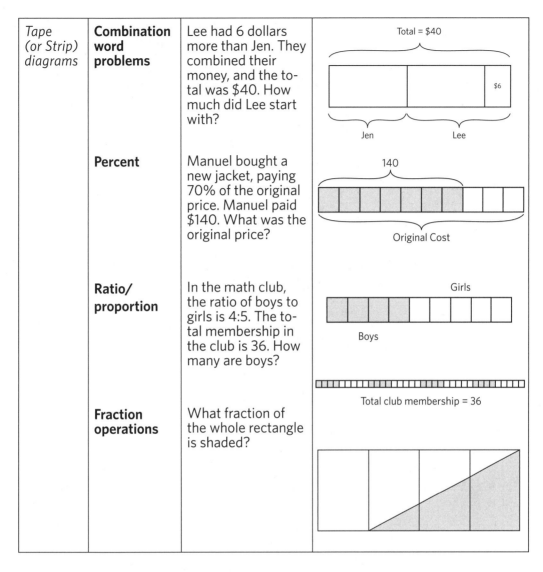

| Tape (or Strip) diagrams | Combination word problems | Lee had 6 dollars more than Jen. They combined their money, and the total was $40. How much did Lee start with? | Total = $40 ... Jen ... Lee ... $6 |
| | Percent | Manuel bought a new jacket, paying 70% of the original price. Manuel paid $140. What was the original price? | 140 ... Original Cost |
| | Ratio/ proportion | In the math club, the ratio of boys to girls is 4:5. The total membership in the club is 36. How many are boys? | Girls ... Boys ... Total club membership = 36 |
| | Fraction operations | What fraction of the whole rectangle is shaded? | |

You may wonder why we omit circle diagrams from the table. Circle diagrams can be very helpful in representing and understanding part-whole relationships. However, students can overgeneralize their usefulness. Drawing a circle diagram requires some precision in depicting parts, which in turn requires some conceptual understanding about angle size. Many middle graders, in our experience, do not yet have that kind of understanding of angle. Thus, for a task that began "A box contains both red and green apples. $3/7$ of the apples are red . . ." we saw many students struggle to divide a circle into seven approximately equal parts. So, while circle diagrams can serve students well in some topics, their usefulness does not generalize to all topics.

In this chart, we do not include examples of visual representations of geometric reasoning. Omitting geometric drawings from this chart does not represent any de-emphasis by us on this important form of visual representation. Rather, geometric representations are not as easily classified as quantitative/algebraic representations, so we have not included them in this classification chart. Beyond the conventional ways of representing spatial relationships, like congruence, geometric task solvers often are left to their own devices to represent their reasoning. This is particularly true when reasoning includes geometric transformations. For example, you may recall from Chapter 2 how Mario used shading and arrows to convey his intention to cut and rotate pieces of the given triangle.

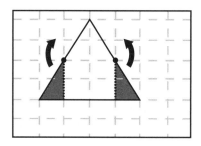

Try matching a task with a visual representation for yourself. Read the following task. What visual representation(s) would you use or expect students to use?

---

### The Choir Problem

In a choir containing boys and girls, 55% are boys. There are 4 more boys than girls. How many children are there altogether? Explain your thinking, first in pictures, then in words.

---

What visual representation did you choose? How was that choice helpful to your thinking? Personal preference can enter in. For example, some people prefer comparing areas in tape or array diagrams over comparing number magnitudes in number lines and vice versa.

## Making Visual Representations a Habit

As we have noted, we observed in our work that many, if not most, U.S. middle graders do not use visual representations very often. This applies to English learners as well as native English speakers. The reasons are not clear. It could be due to lack of skill or lack of experience, or it may be due to their having developed the conviction that "math equals computation." (A student in a class we were observing raised his hand and said to the teacher, rather proudly, it seemed, "Miss, I didn't use diagramming. I used math!")

Most likely, the real reason for scant use of visual representations is a combination of all of these—lack of skill, lack of experience, and a narrow mind-set about what constitutes "doing math." With that in mind, and recognizing that many teachers like to begin their lessons with what are often called "Do Nows" or perhaps "Warm-Ups," we see a convenient way to build student habits and skills in mathematical visual representations. On a regular basis, try using this Do Now chunk of time to challenge students with brief encounters with visual representations. We offer several examples:

1.

*Where in the diagram do you see the ratio 2:3 represented? Where do you see 5:3 represented? Where do you see 40% represented? 150%?*

2.

*Look at each visual representation in the following table and decide how the visual representation shows the relationship "**five more than**." Describe each one in writing, then share your thinking with your partner.*

|  | Visual Representation | The visual representation shows the relationship "five more than" |
|---|---|---|
| **A** | 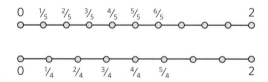 |  |
| **B** |  |  |

3.

*The following diagram shows that ⁴/₅ is closer to 1 than ⁵/₄ is. Discuss with your partner how the diagram shows this.*

4.

*Discuss with your partner how you could use the diagram below to find a fraction that is between ³/₄ and ⁵/₆:*

5.

*In the geometric figure below, reflect point A over line segment BC. Label the new point D. You will now have quadrilateral ABDC. Show at least* **two different ways** *to find the area of quadrilateral ABDC.*

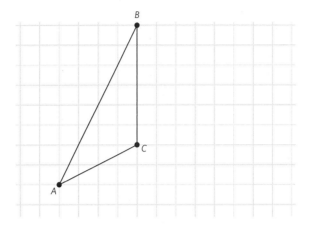

6.

*The rectangle below contains a dark gray triangle and a light gray triangle:*

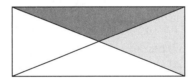

*Compare the area of the dark gray triangle with the area of the light gray triangle. What did you find?*

*Now, in the rectangle below, compare the area of the dark gray triangle with the area of the light gray triangle:*

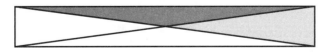

*What did you find? Will this also work on all rectangles? Explain your answer.*

We have used these Do Nows with teachers in our professional development sessions. They generally prompt many analytical reflections about visual representations, for which reason you and your colleagues might consider working on and discussing these Do Nows together in department meetings or study groups. At the same time, these brief tasks have considerable benefit for middle graders to work on, especially EL students. All six of these Do Now candidate tasks likely can be done in fifteen or twenty minutes by middle graders. You may want to alter the levels of challenge if you find some take more than twenty minutes. In any event, our goal for your students is that they get a steady diet of reasoning about visual representations like these in mathematics. Try using them frequently. If you already use Do Nows to begin your lessons, try occasionally making them visual representation Do Nows.

You can also adapt these tasks to provide more options. For example, in Example 1, change to a different tape diagram, say, divided into 7 or 8 or 12 equal sections. Then ask the same kinds of questions. In Examples 3 and 4, change the fraction pairs. In Example 5, there is nothing sacred about using this triangle, or even about using any triangle. Use other figures. In Example 6, try other rectangles; then change the figure to a parallelogram with dark gray and light gray triangles lying on the diagonal. Keep doing variations on the task (once a week, say) until students have agreed on some argument why the equal areas always happen for rectangles and parallelograms.

The following task is likely more time-demanding than a typical Do Now, because it reverses what we usually prompt: *Given a task, draw a diagram to help you solve it. Instead, this one asks, in effect: Given a diagram, what could be a task that inspired it?* Nonetheless, if you want to take more time with it, you can challenge your students with it. (It also can create both energy and enlightenment when teachers work on it together.) In our experience, this reverse process—"Here is the diagram, find the problem"—requires thinking more deeply about different quantitative relationships a given diagram may represent:

7.

*The diagram below can help us solve many different word problems. With a partner, write a word problem that this diagram can help us solve.*

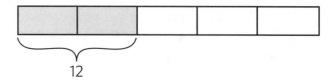

# Conclusion: Creating and Revising Tasks

Look back at the Parallelogram problem on page 14 of Chapter 1. We went through a large handful of revisions on that task before we smoothed out most of the kinks in it. Granted, its purpose was research, and hence needed to stand alone without instructional supports. However, the message from our experience does generalize: For a task to help fulfill learners' mathematical thinking potential, it likely needs a few rounds of testing, revising, and polishing. This may seem costly in terms of time investment, but the chances are good that, in the long run, such vetted tasks can be used over and over again—always, of course, with an eye on the particular purposes for which they are being used.

Let's assume you have a candidate task to use with students from your curriculum or elsewhere, and you are aware of the *purpose* you want the task to serve. Purpose is central to the work of choosing or developing a mathematics task. Once purpose is clear, you should weigh the candidate task against the six *principles* of task design, and they may guide you to determine whether the task will elicit use of visual representations and use of mathematical communication, particularly by ELs, and how you might want to adapt the task to your purpose. Collect the student work, then analyze ELs' student work to look for evidence of mathematical competence and the potential for proficiency, as well as evidence that can improve your instruction.

Once you have identified a task that supports students' use of visual representations and planned language supports to go with it, how do you foster students' ability to approach such a task effectively, particularly if English is not their first language? We believe this requires lesson planning and implementation with attention to goals informed by attention to mathematics content, language, and use of visual representations. In Chapter 1, we laid out our four design principles, the fourth one of which is "Repeated structure practices." In the next chapter, we present instructional routines that embody this principle and help create access for EL students to engage in productive mathematical thinking and communication.

# Chapter 6

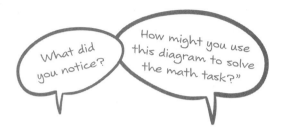

# Visual Representation Routine

Now that we have outlined the importance of and some strategies for supporting ELs' access through visual representations and language supports and discussed criteria for effective tasks, we turn to instructional routines that implement all these ideas. As we discussed in Chapter 1, routines support both students and teachers by reducing the cognitive effort required for the mechanics of a lesson, freeing up energy to focus on how and what the students are learning.

## Overview of the Visual Representations Routine

The Visual Representations Routine described below supports student learning about the use of diagrams and geometric drawings to work on mathematics problems as described in Chapter 2 while integrating language strategies described in Chapter 4. Students learn to use diagrams to represent important quantities and relationships as a means for making sense of number and algebra questions, and they learn to use geometric drawings to reveal properties and relationships that are important in geometric situations. The routine can be paired with any mathematical task that requires students to engage in mathematical reasoning and lends itself to creating and using visual representations to solve the task.

## Creating and Analyzing Visual Representations

The routine has two versions, each of which is intended to develop students' skills and understanding about how to create and use visual representations to work on mathematics tasks. The creating version of the routine provides students opportunities to work on creating their own visual representations to solve mathematics problems, while the analyzing version supports students' analysis of existing visual representations. The analyzing version complements the creating version by providing support for students to learn about strategies for creating visual representations. We developed the analyzing version of the routine when we were working with collaborating teachers who pointed out that many students had so little background in creating visual representations that they were getting stuck on how to begin working. By engaging with the two complementary versions of this routine, students can develop their own ability to create and use visual representations, aided by opportunities to think deeply about how provided visual representations have been used. We encourage moving back and forth between opportunities for students to create diagrams and geometric drawings and opportunities for students to analyze provided examples.

## Routine Structure

The routine comprises four parts:

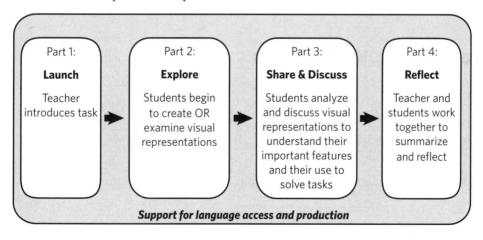

*Part I—Launch:* Teacher introduces mathematics task, supports language access, and prepares students for the routine.

*Part II—Explore:* Students work on creating or understanding visual representations and using them to solve the mathematics task, with support for language production. In the creating version of the routine, students will be generating their own diagrams or geometric drawings to discuss together in Part III, while in the analyzing version of the routine students examine sample visual representations to then discuss during Part III.

*Part III—Share and Discuss:* As a class, students analyze and discuss visual representations (that they created or the sample visual representations that they analyzed) to understand their important features and their use to solve mathematics tasks, with support for language production.

*Part IV—Reflect:* Teacher summarizes key ideas and students consider and share what they have learned about the use of visual representations to solve mathematics tasks.

## Support for Student Language Access and Production

Throughout the routine, key academic language related to the mathematics and the task context is surfaced, defined, and used by students to communicate their mathematical thinking. The routine incorporates mechanisms (e.g., pairs work, sentence starters) that support access to language and production of language by students who are English learners. At key moments in the routine, teachers are asked to insert additional appropriate language access and language production strategies tailored to the particular mathematics task and/or the English language proficiency levels of students who will engage with the task.

# Routine Implementation

Earlier we described the overall structure of the routine. Here we provide detailed instructions and support notes for planning and implementing the different parts of the routine with mathematics tasks so that students can develop their ability to create and use visual representations to solve mathematics problems. In portions of the routine where the creating and analyzing versions differ, the instructions and notes split into two columns.

| Creating Version | Analyzing Version |
|---|---|
| **Part I—Launch** ||

1. ***Display and explain the purpose and process of the routine to students.***
   - The central purpose of the routine is to learn how to use visual representations to solve and communicate about mathematical tasks.
2. ***Distribute or display mathematics task, and use appropriate language access strategies*** (e.g., Three Reads) to ensure that all students understand the task context and instructions.

| Creating Version | Analyzing Version |
|---|---|
|  | 2a. Orient students to sample visual representations. |
|  | • Explain that the series of pictures shows how another student created a diagram. It shows the steps the student took. |
|  | • Display complete visual strip. With their pencils down, have students look at the strip for fifteen to thirty seconds. Ask "What do you notice?" Record responses, pointing to the visual or having students point at the visual to indicate what they are noticing. |
|  | • Next, display the strip again, but this time revealing one step at a time. As each new step comes into view, ask students to turn and talk to a partner about what changed from the previous step to the newly revealed step. Students do not need to consider why the visual representation changed, just what is different in the new step from the previous one. For each new step, after some partner discussion, one or two students could share an idea about what is different in the full group, being sure to point at the displayed visual representation when sharing. |
|  | • Create a Co-constructed Word Bank by eliciting from students words or phrases they think will be important to help describe the sample student work and adding additional words or phrases yourself. |

*Continued*

| Creating Version | Analyzing Version |
|---|---|
| **Part II—Individual/Pairs Work** ||
| 3. *Individual work.* **Give students one to two minutes to work individually on creating a visual representation for the task.** | 3. *Individual work.* **Give students one to two minutes to work individually to complete the sentence starter "I wonder . . ." about the sample student's work.** |
| The goal is to learn about using diagrams or geometric drawings to solve mathematics tasks, so students should not use a nonvisual method to solve the task right now.<br>• One or two minutes is not enough time to finish, but it is enough time to generate starting ideas to then share with a partner.<br>• Circulate but do not intervene unless you planned to support access to task instructions for individual students. ||
| 4. *Pairs work.* **Give students about eight minutes to work in pairs.** Tell students to:<br><br>(a) share the visual representations they started,<br><br>(b) identify and discuss how these visual representations represent important information from the math task, then<br><br>(c) work together to refine and/or create new visual representations that will help solve the math task. | 4. *Pairs work.* **Give students about eight minutes to work in pairs.** Tell students to:<br><br>(a) share what they noticed and wondered,<br><br>(b) work together to make sense of each step of the sample student's approach, then<br><br>(c) write an explanation of each step of the sample student's approach in the space below each frame on the handout. |
| • Planning tip: Consider how to support *language production* (e.g., strategic partnering, word bank, sentence starters, interview questions) for this pairs work.<br>• Circulate and ask questions that model academic language use, and assess student understanding of the task. Examples (adapt to number/algebra or geometry tasks):<br>  ◦ How does this diagram (*geometric drawing*) represent [insert important quantity, relationship, or property of figure here]?<br>  ◦ What is a new [quantity, relationship, property, etc.] that you notice in your diagram (*geometric drawing*) that wasn't given in the task?<br>  ◦ How might you use this diagram (*geometric drawing*) to solve the math task?<br>  ◦ For number/algebra: What does that number represent?<br>  ◦ For geometry: Why did you add that line? Transform that shape? ||

| Part II—Individual/Pairs Work | |
|---|---|
| 5. While they are working in pairs, identify a range of diagrams/geometric drawing to display for students to discuss during Part III (the sharing/analyzing portion of the routine). You can supplement students' visual representations with ones you prepared in advance. Choose visual representations to:<br><br>• Show a range of representations and highlight different characteristics of useful diagrams as well as aspects of diagrams that are not helpful in understanding or providing entry points to the math task.<br><br>• Show how diagramming can be a "thinking tool" that shows the development of thinking and may not yet be drawn precisely, not just a "presentation of a solution" (which would be a cleaned up representation of the final relationships that were discovered for communication to others). The diagrams also do not need to be "complete." You can choose to share only a portion of a student's diagramming work. | 5. While they are working in pairs, identify student explanations of, and questions about, the sample visual representations to display for students to discuss during Part III (the sharing/analyzing portion of the routine). You may consider the following when selecting students to share:<br><br>• Select different students to explain what is happening in different steps of the sample visual representation. This will allow different students to communicate about the mathematics, even if they could not all make sense of all of the steps of the visual representation.<br><br>• Select students to share who have alternative interpretations of what is happening in the sample visual representation.<br><br>• Select students to share who have identified ways to change the visual representation or who have open questions about how to use the visual representation to solve the given problem or extensions of the problem. |
| **Part III—Sharing/Discussing** | |
| 6. *Repeated cycles of think/pair/share for different students' visual representations:* Display multiple visual representations one at a time, and for each one, have students individually consider what they notice (30 seconds), discuss with a partner what they noticed and how the displayed visual representation represents important information (2 minutes), and then share ideas in the full group.<br><br>• For the first visual representation, you may wish to skip the *pair* step and go straight to *full group* if students in the class need support understanding what they might notice. | 6. *Full-group discussion about the visual representations in sample work:* Display the steps from the sample visual representation one at a time, and for each one, have one or two students share ideas about what the sample student did with the visual representation in that step. Lead a discussion of how the student may have used the visual representation to solve the mathematical problem or what other questions can be answered with that visual representation. |

*Continued*

| Creating Version | Analyzing Version |
|---|---|
| **Part III—Sharing/Discussing** | |
| • Have students point to the displayed diagram or geometric drawing to illustrate ideas that they share. Annotate the diagram with student observations, and invite clarifying questions from students.<br>• As students share ideas in the full group, begin recording characteristics of helpful diagrams or geometric drawings identified by students, and add to that list with each new displayed visual representation. | |
| 7. *Full-group identifying characteristics:* After reviewing several visual representations, ask students to share in the full group about the following to generate characteristics: *Which diagrams/geometric drawing(s) helped you understand the math task? How did that diagram/geometric drawing help you think about how to solve the question in the math task?* | 7. *Full-group identifying characteristics:* After reviewing all steps of the sample visual representation, ask students to share in the full group about the following to generate characteristics: *How did that diagram/geometric drawing help you think about how to solve the question in the math task?* |
| **Part IV—Summary/Reflection** | |
| 8. *Display one or more Sentence Starters and Frames, and ask students to individually write a complete sentence using a sentence starter/frame.*<br> ○ Diagramming a word problem helps me to understand . . .<br> ○ The next time I diagram a word problem I will include . . . because . . .<br> ○ An important characteristic of a useful diagram is . . . because . . .<br>9. *Have students read their completed sentence frame to a partner.*<br>10. *Ask several students to share their reflection(s) with the whole class.*<br> • Remind students that the goal is not to get the answer or identify the best diagram or geometric drawing but to learn more about how to create/analyze diagrams and geometric drawings. Remembering the numerical answer to the problem won't help them in the future, but a better understanding of how to use diagrams and visuals to solve problems will be useful.<br> • Tailor the sentence starters and frames to your students' English language proficiency levels. | |

Overall, you can see that the analyzing version of the routine has much the same structure and purpose as the creating version of the routine. The key differences all connect to the idea that in the analyzing version, students start by analyzing a provided visual representation rather than producing their own. So, in the *Launch*, students need to orient themselves to the provided visual representation so they are prepared to analyze it—paying attention to what they notice about each of the steps that the problem solver took to produce that visual representation (and in particular, orienting themselves to what visual changes happen between steps). In addition, we emphasize the use of the Co-constructed Word Bank language strategy (see Chapter 4) in the analyzing version because that version has a central focus on students producing language about the mathematics. Therefore, constructing a word bank that includes words both the teacher and students find important, and also asking students to incorporate certain of those words in their work, can be helpful. During *individual/pairs work* students are focused on making sense of the provided visual representation (broken down into steps) rather than creating their own visual representation. The *sharing/discussing* section has the same purpose, in that students will discuss together how a visual representation represents important information from the task and how it is used to solve the task. The key difference is that the visual representation serving as the artifact for discussion is the provided one that all students in the class have been working with, rather than student-constructed ones that their peers have not seen until they get to this section of the routine. Finally, the *reflecting on learning* section of the routine is the same in the creating and analyzing versions because in both cases, students are reflecting on their takeaways about their learning about the use of visual representations as mathematical problem-solving tools.

Teachers with whom we have collaborated have used the routine periodically with their students throughout the school year each time paired with a different mathematics task. They have found it helpful to use the creating version of the routine on a regular basis so that students begin to develop habits of thinking related to creating visual representations. In addition, interspersing periodic opportunities to engage with the analyzing version of the routine provides a mechanism for introducing students to new ideas and strategies related to creating and using visual representations.

## Example: Creating Version

As an example, let's consider how the creating version looks when implemented for the How Many People? task (introduced in earlier chapters).

---

### How Many People?

The population of the town of Medtown is three times the size of the population of the town of Carburg.

The *difference* in the number of people in the two towns is 2,184 people.

How many people live in Medtown and Carburg **combined**?

Create a diagram that helps you to solve the problem. Show your work.

---

During the *launch* of this task the teacher might use the Three Reads strategy (see Chapter 4) to help students become familiar with (1) the context of this task about town populations, (2) the question they are trying to answer in the task, and then (3) the important information provided in the problem. The teacher may employ the Clarifying Vocabulary strategy to help students understand what words such as *combined* mean, perhaps having other students act out *combining* or provide synonyms for the word. During the individual/pairs work on the task, students would be tasked with creating diagrams that represent the important information they identified during the Three Reads (e.g., Medtown's population is three times Carburg's population; 2,184 more people live in Medtown than Carburg) and trying to use the diagrams to solve the task. During the pairs work, the teacher might provide students with sentence starters or questions to ask each other about the diagrams they started during individual time, such as "My diagram shows the population of Carburg by . . ." or "Where does your diagram show the difference between the two towns?" The teacher would circulate during pairs work to ask students questions about the quantities and relationships that are included in their diagrams and to identify a few diagrams to share with the whole class. The teacher moves on to a full-group sharing of diagrams without worrying about whether all (or even most) students have a complete diagram that can be used to solve the task. Her purpose during this routine is to support students' developing understanding of how to create mathematical diagrams that will help them solve tasks. In this case, finding the numerical answer to the task is not her primary concern, but helping students examine the diagrams of their peers and figure out how those diagrams are helpful to solving the task and perhaps identifying together as a class ways to build from those diagrams to solve the task are her main goals for the students. Perhaps one of the student diagrams that she asks a student to share looks like this example:

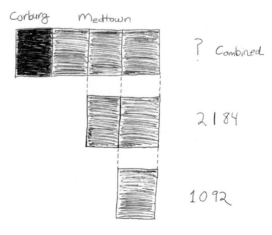

While the student's work is projected using a document camera, the teacher could ask the class to consider "Where do you see the 'three times' represented? Where do you see the difference between the populations of the two towns? Where do you see the combined populations?" After discussing several different diagrams during this *sharing/discussing* section of the routine, the teacher would have all students reflect on their learning about diagrams from the day's lesson in the *reflecting on learning* section of the routine. Examples of what students have written in their reflections on learning include:

- The next time I diagram a word problem I will . . .

  ° Try to include all of the information and relationships. *[This student may have noticed the value in representing the important values or relationships between values in the diagram in order to aid in solving the task.]*

  ° Make boxes and try cutting them apart. *[This student may have experienced tape diagrams during the lesson and is at the beginning stages of making sense of how to use them.]*

(Note: For a version of this routine using a geometry task and geometric drawings, reflections might include: "I can change a geometric drawing by making a regular shape like a square"; or "I can change a geometric drawing by rotating it or cutting pieces off and putting them in a different place.") In setting up the reflection on learning, the teacher might remind the students that diagrams are important as problem-solving tools and that she wants them to reflect on what they have learned today about diagrams, because it is far more important that they remember that than it is that they remember the combined population of these two towns from this task. She could have the students write their completed sentence starters on an exit slip and collect them to review before the next class as part of her ongoing efforts to gauge her students' understanding and their ability to express that understanding with language.

## Example: Analyzing Version

The analyzing version of the routine follows much the same sequence of steps as the creating version. However, a key difference is that the primary visual representation artifact that students are working with is a provided visual representation rather than visual representations that students create. The provided visual representation for analysis could be incomplete (students are asked to complete it), partially incorrect (students are asked to determine what is incorrect and correct it), or complete and correct (students are asked to describe the flow of the thinking). Regardless of what type of provided visual representation is given to students, the students have the opportunity to analyze that visual representation and make sense of how someone else could have used it to solve the task.

For example, think back to the Sharing Candies task we've seen several times:

*Sara had a bag of candies.*

*She gave $^1/_3$ of the candies to Raul.*

*Then Sara gave $^1/_4$ of the candies she had left to Jasmine.*

*After giving candies to Raul and Jasmine, Sara had 24 candies left in her bag.*

*How many candies did Sara have at the beginning?*

*Take a moment to think about a diagram you could draw that might help you solve this task.*

Now, look at the work of Janet (a fictitious student) on this task:

---

### Janet's Work on Sharing Candies

---

How many candies did Sara have at the beginning?

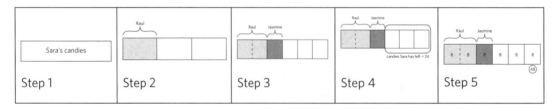

Instead of creating their own diagrams, students are instead asked to analyze and make sense of the steps Janet took (which, in this case are a complete and correct set of steps). This allows the students to learn and reflect on important features of mathematical diagrams. Importantly, we have also found in our early work with implementing the analyzing version of the routine that it promotes significant production of language about the mathematics by students who are ELs, even more than the creating version of the routine or other regular classroom lessons. The provided artifact (a visual representation) provides a talking point for students to describe (and for students to point to, giving them more confidence in their verbal communication abilities). Also, through providing a sample visual representation, the cognitive load of thinking through how to create a new visual representation is reduced and the cognitive load represented by language demands can be raised, and students can expend more energy on being active participants in mathematical communication.

## Planning for Use of the Visual Representations Routine

This routine is intended as a blueprint for designing lessons that create access for all students to challenging mathematics, especially as represented in the Common Core Standards of Mathematical Practice. It relies on use of mathematical visual representations, woven together with language access and language production strategies. The routine can be used on a regular basis with different mathematics tasks (and in cases where the analyzing version is used, with different sample visual representations).

When planning how to implement the routine with a particular mathematics task, consider these questions:

- What is your goal for mathematical learning for students?

- What is your objective for students in relation to mathematical language and/or communication?

- What language strategies will you use to support language access and language production? How will you use them? (E.g., what words or phrases would you want to emphasize if using the Co-constructed Word Bank? What sentence starters and frames would you use, for whom, and when during the routine? What questions will you ask students as you circulate to advance or assess their thinking, and how will you tailor them based on English language proficiency?)

- Select four focus students of different English language proficiency levels. What do you anticipate these focus students will say or write during the routine that would be in line with your objectives? How will you support those students with accessing and producing language during the routine (i.e., how might you differentiate or tailor these strategies for these students)? (Below is a sample chart you could use as a template for responding to this question. We have included a couple of examples for possible students. These examples are based on the Sharing Candies task introduced earlier.)

| Student(s) | ELP | Examples of Written or Spoken Language in Line with Objectives | Ways You Will Use or Differentiate/Tailor Language Access/ Production Strategies for These Students |
|---|---|---|---|
| Carlos | Beginner | Raul's candy and Jasmine's candy and Sara's 24 pieces of candy is the total.<br><br>Here is Raul's candy. (pointing at diagram)<br><br>Raul's candy is two squares. Jasmine's candy is one square. | Act out the Sharing Candies scenario additional times with Carlos' small group with particular emphasis on what is happening when the word *left* comes up.<br><br>During sharing, use a sentence starter such as "My diagram shows Raul's candy by . . ." repeatedly with each person who shares, so that Carlos can pick up the pattern, and then have Carlos try it for his diagram. |
| Mei | Intermediate | Raul has two times Jasmine's candies.<br><br>Raul has 8 more candies than Jasmine.<br><br>Raul's candies are shown by dividing the rectangle in three parts. | Ask Mei and other students to think of another sentence that uses *left* with the same meaning as in this task.<br><br>Encourage Mei to try to use *more than* when describing how her diagram shows the important information. |

If you are planning to use the creating version of the routine, you will need to consider the task with which you are using the routine and then answer the questions above, thinking through each step in the routine and what it will look like for that task—e.g., anticipating the kinds of responses and drawings that students may generate and the support they may need. Chapter 5 provided guidance about selecting appropriate tasks for this kind of routine. One additional question to consider during planning a creating version of the routine is whether or not to include a question for the task. While a task will usually have a question associated with it, and the purpose of creating a visual representation is to help answer that question, it can also be valuable to have students create diagrams or geometric drawings that represent the important information in a task context and then think about what mathematical questions they can answer with that visual representation.

If you are planning to use the analyzing version of the routine, then you need to select not only a task but also a series of diagramming steps to present to students for analysis. Some examples are provided in this book, but you can also create your own by considering what steps in the diagramming process you want students to examine (and for what type of diagram or geometric drawing). For example, consider how you might fill in the rectangles below to show the steps that Carla (a fictitious student) took to create the diagram shown in Step 4 for this problem:

*Rita read 224 pages of a book. Rita still has ¹/₅ of the book left to read. How many pages are in the book?*

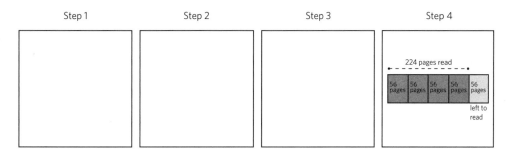

To fill in the steps, consider what you want students to notice about productive strategies for getting started. For example, think through what Step 1 will show. It may represent one important piece of information from the problem, or it may represent two. Or, consider what will change between each pair of steps in order to show students how a diagram can progress as a thinking tool and how it relates to the important information in the task. If you are not sure how to get started creating steps, think about how you would diagram the task, and if possible share and discuss with colleagues so you can see alternative approaches. You do not need to limit yourself to four steps if you want to break the process down more or less. Keep in mind that every step in the process does not need to end up represented in one of the boxes.

Whether using a creating version of the routine or an analyzing version, the intention is that students develop their understanding of what diagrams and geometric drawings can look like; how they relate to the information about quantities, properties, and/or relationships given in a task; and how they are useful for working on solving mathematical problems or answering mathematical questions. If students are given enough opportunities to really dive into understanding and valuing the use of mathematical representations, they will be better equipped to use visual representations in other mathematical problem-solving situations. Furthermore, to provide maximum benefit to ELs, it is important to attend carefully to the opportunities within the routine for integrating support for language access and language production. This allows students full access to the benefits of participating in the routine. We have also seen students pick up on language strategies embedded in the routine and begin to transfer them to other settings as self-supports for language as well—such as using a version of the Three Reads strategy to help themselves interpret mathematics tasks in other lessons or on standardized tests. Students may benefit from explicit reminders that what they are learning within these routines about visual representations and about making sense of mathematics tasks are important tools for all of their mathematical problem solving, to help them transfer this learning to their everyday lessons.

# Chapter 7

# Putting It All into Practice

In this final chapter, we summarize some starting places, allowing teachers to enrich their current practice in ways that create access for EL students to develop proficiency in mathematical reasoning, mathematical practices, and mathematical communication. We also examine how this kind of work can be brought into professional development and professional learning. While this latter topic is of most importance to coaches and professional developers, we hope individual teachers will be inspired to push for this kind of professional learning opportunity as well.

## Bringing These Ideas to Your Classroom Instruction

This book has offered different adaptations you can apply to the lesson planning, delivery, and debriefing you already do in the classroom, intended to help ELs become more mathematically productive in your lessons. In that light, the best starting place for trying the ideas in this book is to *plan a lesson, try it out, and see what you can learn from how students think and communicate about the tasks in the lesson.* You can do that work on your own, but we believe it is more effective to engage one or two colleagues to join you and to be your consultants in planning and debriefing. Ideally, ESL specialists and mathematics teachers could collaborate on this work.

The following list may help you in this process.

1. *Build student understanding of, and habits of using, visual representations.* In this book we have described how all students in middle grades—especially, but not only, EL students—can benefit from learning how to use visual representations as mathematical thinking tools. In Chapter 5, we showed examples of brief visual representation tasks, resembling what many teachers call Do Nows or Math Warm-Ups, as a key tool for building this capacity in students. In Chapter 6, we laid out a longer Visual Representations Routine that can be paired with a variety of mathematics tasks to develop students' understanding of visual representations. We recommend doing these tasks with students regularly in order to deepen students' understanding of how to use visual representations, such as diagrams, as mathematical thinking tools. Regular engagement in these activities can build habits for students of appealing to visual representations when faced with other challenging mathematical tasks.

2. *Select and adapt mathematics tasks to elicit productive mathematical struggle on the part of all students, as well as practice their use of visual representations as thinking tools.* In Chapter 1, we made the case for using mathematics tasks that require students to do real mathematical work, that is, mathematical reasoning and problem solving, and we addressed what that kind of work looks like in Chapters 3 and 5. Your curriculum materials likely have examples of such tasks. Numerous sources of such tasks exist online, including these three examples:

   https://www.illustrativemathematics.org

   http://mathandlanguage.edc.org

   http://mathpractices.edc.org

   The second and third of these were developed with colleagues during work with, respectively, teachers wanting to help students who are ELs in mathematics, and teachers interested in understanding how to tap the Common Core Mathematical Practices. There are many additional websites with helpful collections of tasks. These three can be a start.

3. *Use the language access and language production strategies described in Chapter 4.* Try using language support strategies not only when using the Visual Representation Routine but also in other lesson activities you plan. For example, when a lesson involves a word problem, take five extra minutes and employ the Three Reads strategy. Or, in your use of Do Nows with visual representations, prompt responses in writing, using Sentence Starters and Frames. For example, the following is one of the suggested Do Nows from Chapter 6:

   *Discuss with your partner how you could use the diagram below to find a fraction that is between $3/4$ and $5/6$:*

   Instead of relying only on the open prompt, "Discuss with your partner," one could add the sentence starters:

   "To use the diagram to find a fraction between $3/4$ and $5/6$, first we . . ."

   "Next, we . . ."

   Furthermore, learn about your students so that you can choose and use language support strategies appropriately. What are students' English language proficiency levels? What other languages do students speak that could serve as a resource? Are the students proficient in reading and writing in those other languages?

4. *Practice identifying the Standards for Mathematical Practice in your own mathematical work and in students' mathematical work.* The website cited above, http://mathpractices.edc.org, has activities to orient teachers to the eight mathematical practices, and what they can look and sound like in mathematical work. Use the student-work analysis template from Chapter 3 (pp. 55–57) to examine your students' work for evidence of the practices in the form of students' mathematical reasoning and their mathematical communication. It's helpful to remember that much of middle-grade mathematics relates to quantities, spatial properties, and problems involving quantitative and spatial relationships. This fact lends special prominence to two of the eight standards: SMP 2, *Reason abstractly and quantitatively*, and SMP 7, *Look for and make use of structure*, which both relate to identifying

and making sense of these quantities, properties, and relationships. When focused on using visual representations, learners also regularly employ SMP 1, *Make sense of problems and persevere in solving them*, and SMP 5, *Use appropriate tools strategically* through the process of exploring and solving tasks with the support of visual representations. And, when students revise their diagrams in their written task responses, this can provide evidence of the "persevere in solving them" part of the SMP 1 description. Similarly, when learners are careful to ensure that their visual representations and words convey clearly their thinking, they are employing SMP 6, *Attend to precision*. When they use visual representations to build an argument about a relationship in a task or to critique someone else's argument, this is in line with SMP 3, *Construct viable arguments and critique the reasoning of others*. SMP 4 and 8 may appear as well, depending on the nature of the task. Our point here is to make clear that SMP 1, 3, 5, and 6 are easier to see when mathematical visual representations and mathematical language are parts of the task responses, and SMP 2 and 7 arise because of the nature of many of the tasks encountered in middle grades.

## Using These Ideas in Professional Learning

Like many other educators, we think of learning—at all ages—as *meaning making*, for instance, middle-grade students making meaning of the different representations of rational numbers and how they connect to each other; or tying spatial concepts to the various words and phrases that constitute the language of geometric reasoning. Learning is also, in good part, a *social practice*, with learners learning from each other, as much as they learn on their own, along with practicing inquiry and argumentation together, to sharpen their disciplinary skills.

As a social practice, learning in professional development can include *solving professional problems collaboratively*. For us, a prime example of this occurred while we were leading professional development in New York City with school teams that included mathematics coaches, ESL specialists, assistant principals, and mathematics teachers. In between seminars, these teams would collect student work on geometric reasoning tasks done by EL students, then bring the student work to the following seminar, where they would analyze the work together, before doing team planning for instruction. Over the course of the year, these efforts amounted to collaborative solving of several EL-related problems, not the least of which was the problem that there had been little schoolwide ownership felt across schools on how to provide ELs access to quality learning. This experience highlighted the importance of collaboration when striving to best meet the needs of ELs and of all students.

In summary, we concluded, our role as professional developers is to create:

- Opportunities for meaning making

- Opportunities for social learning

- Experiences for engaging with mathematics as a discipline with its own norms of inquiry and argumentation

- Tools for solving important professional problems in schools and districts, especially those related to instruction;  for example, teachers in schools can solve the problem of inadequate attention to the needs of EL students.

## Grounding Professional Development and Learning in the Classroom

Group seminar series, like the ones we have led for teachers in New York City and elsewhere, can go a long way toward satisfying the first three bullet points listed earlier. However, when it comes to the fourth point, we found we needed to add a second prong to the group learning in the seminars. Group sessions can describe and model instructional tools, but to best support guiding implementation into the classroom, it is important to provide another set of eyes and ears to do structured observations and debriefings of the tools being implemented. We believe this coaching role is the missing piece in efforts to create a "win-win" solution, where teachers are doing things differently, not just doing *more* things.

We refer to what Atul Gawande[1] described as the "sort of coaching that fosters effective innovation and judgment, not merely the replication of technique" (2011, 51). A designated school or district mathematics coach fits this bill nicely, but we recognize that the current economics of schooling do not allow many schools to have full-time, or even part-time, coaches to guide teachers. With these realities in mind, but still wanting to achieve coaching that fosters effective innovation and judgment, in our work we have implemented a model of coaching that allows peers to coach each other in ways that focus

---

[1]  Atul Gawande, "Annals of Medicine: Personal Best," *The New Yorker* (October 3, 2011): 44–53.

on innovation and judgment, while also enriching the guidance by involving official school mathematics coaches, where those roles exist.

The coaching of teachers of EL students that we have used is intended to support the implementation of the routine described in Chapter 6 as well as other ideas from this book that can be explored in professional development seminars. Specifically, we encourage a collaborative and evidence-driven approach to using the routine whereby a coach or other colleague can participate in discussions with the teacher enacting the routine both before and after implementation of the routine. The coach or colleague collects evidence about students' engagement with the routine during the lesson to share and discuss with the teacher. We encourage a focus on student evidence that includes artifacts of ELs' reasoning, problem solving, and use of academic language. We call this cycle of collaborative discussions before and after implementation of the routine (or any other routine) a *classroom inquiry cycle* (CIC).

CICs are structured in a way that should be familiar to teachers who have worked with a mathematics coach. The CIC begins when the teacher creates a plan for implementing an instructional routine in his/her classroom that was introduced in a seminar session. The teacher then meets with the facilitator to review the teacher's plan. Teachers participating in CICs may make small adjustments to their plan for implementing an instructional routine between the seminar session and the CIC. While it is desirable for the facilitator to be available to support teachers in this planning, we recognize that may not always be feasible.

The facilitator observes the teacher's implementation of the routine while gathering data about students' mathematical work and mathematical communication. After the lesson, the teacher and facilitator review the evidence related to engagement by students who are ELs in the routine and select student work samples to bring to the next seminar session.

The facilitator is "another pair of eyes and ears" in the classroom, gathering evidence of student reasoning and language use, especially by ELs. The facilitator is *not* in the classroom to evaluate the teacher nor to serve as an additional teacher. Protocols for CICs make this distinction clear and are provided in the professional development materials associated with this book (*see sidebar*).

The "coach" (or facilitator of the CIC) in this model has the role of:

- helping teachers to consolidate, in their instruction, the implications of what they are learning in the seminars;

- in particular, helping them become more technically expert in using the seminar-based language strategies in their instruction;

- working together with teachers to internalize the meaning of the Standards of Mathematical Practice and their implications for teaching practice;

> **How to Access the Online Professional Development Resources**
>
> Step 1: Go to www.heinemann.com
>
> Step 2: Click on "Login" to open or create your account. Enter your email address and password or click "Create a New Account" to set up an account.
>
> Step 3: Enter keycode MTACPD and click "Register."

- supporting teachers to advance the use of visual representations, like diagrams, to complement verbal-based learning of mathematics;

- gathering evidence from lessons of ELs' use of mathematical language and visual representations;

- collaborating with teachers to analyze such evidence, not only for signs of need but also for signs of growing competence in language and mathematics;

- further, collaborating with teachers to use the evidence to hone their skills in asking questions that assess and advance student mathematical reasoning.

The professional development materials that accompany this book (available at www.heinemann.com) can support you as you move into productive practice and as you work on your professional learning. These materials include guidelines and handouts for several teacher seminars where exploring the ideas and tasks from this book are central.

# Conclusion

Throughout this book we have described principles, strategies, and examples that we have found useful to support ELs in the mathematics classroom. We hope that we have left you with images of the power of visual representations as mathematical thinking tools and with many ideas about how to weave support for both language access and language production into your mathematics lessons. Most of all we hope that we have left you as eager as we are to help every student be an active participant in the work and fun of doing and discussing mathematics.